CAUGHT FROM TIME

CAUGHT FROM TIME

'All had their beauty, their bright moments' gift,
Their something caught from Time, the ever-swift'
John Masefield

A Country Diary of the 1920s

by

Anne Garnett

TABB HOUSE
Padstow   Cornwall

First published 1986
by Tabb House, 11 Church Street, Padstow, Cornwall

Printed and Bound in Great Britain by
T. J. Press (Padstow) Ltd, Padstow, Cornwall

FOR THE FEW WHO REMAIN
ESPECIALLY REX

LIST OF CONTENTS

ACKNOWLEDGEMENTS

I WOULD LIKE to thank those of my friends who encouraged me to look again at my journals with a view to publication, in particular Mr and Mrs Rex Sangar, and the late Mrs Joan Kerr, the Joan Davy of the diaries. She wrote in 1974 'the Taunton-Minehead railway! You remember the journeys we had in those far-off days, and how every station seemed to have its own drama. I wish you would try to write about it.' Of course I had, in these old diaries.

My grateful thanks are due to Mrs Allanson Bailey for the photograph of her father, Mr Wood; to Mr Floyd of Alcombe for those chosen from his splendid collection, i.e. the Indian Polo Team at Dunster, Horner Woods, Porlock Weir, and a meet of the hounds at St Andries, also to Mr Bawdon for the two photographs of meets of the Devon and Somerset Staghounds in the days when his father was Huntsman.

My acknowledgement is also due to the Dorset Natural History and Archaeological Society, Dorset County Museum, Dorchester, for the photograph of Symondsbury; and for their help in providing information my thanks to Mr Ron Hayes, Mr John Jordan of the BBC Written Archives Centre, Ms Eleanor Hamlyn of the Auckland Public Library, New Zealand, and the Cornwall County Reference Librarian.

Anne Garnett

LIST OF PLATES

Colour Sketches

Photographs

FOREWORD

ANNE GARNETT was fourteen when in 1922 she was suspected of being tubercular. A specialist advised country air and she was despatched with her governess 'AVS' to farmhouse lodgings in West Somerset.

It was a familiar life, as AVS' father, until his retirement a few years before, had been Rector of Elworthy, a straggling parish under the Brendon Hills. Anne had often stayed at the Rectory and at the next-door Whites Farm, and her family had spent several holidays in the neighbourhood until in 1920 Robert, Anne's father, took a house in Dorset. From then on they moved there every spring and summer from their house in West Hill, Highgate.

The specialist thought Anne's convalescence might take two years. Now, in 1925, her family thought it time for her to return to London. However, recurrent attacks of illness made AVS reluctant to consent, which caused friction, as relatives assured the Garnett parents that Anne was 'running wild among all those rustics' and that the governess's influence was altogether too strong.

AVS' influence was not confined to Anne — she exercised it strongly upon Matty Garnett, who, much occupied in literary projects, thought that 'Nanny is usually right about children' and submitted.

Her other four were already grown up; the daughters Narney and Rayne, twenty-five and twenty-three, the boys Richard and Robin, twenty-one and eighteen. Rayne was already married, Narney nursing, Richard in his father's firm of solicitors, and Robin in the Canadian Mounted Police.

In their house of books, Robert and Matty were perhaps relieved at the absence of AVS. Uniting a strong Church of England faith with an even stronger belief in her own rectitude, this remarkable woman failed dismally — apart from her devotion to her employers and affection for Anne — in human relationships. Under her sway at West Hill the girls bore her admonitions with what patience they could muster, servants departed as soon as they decently could, and the boys detested her. All agreed, however, that she was 'wonderful with children'.

1

AVS' attitude to 'the lower orders' made frequent changings in lodgings inevitable. First settled at Whites Farm with the much-loved Hayes family, consisting of Ned, Maggy, their son Gordon, and Ned's old father Isaac, it was not long before AVS fell out with her landlady, and removed Anne to a farm about a mile distant. Here they were warmly cared for by an elderly couple, the Middletons.

The farmer's pony was the first of many that Anne rode and his kisses in the hay-barton the first of that nature she had received. She dealt with the farmer's kisses much as she did the former – something that 'had to be managed'.

Whether AVS became aware of this state of affairs is problematical, but a move was soon made to Stogumber, the ostensible reason being its proximity to the railway and to access to a day-school at Minehead. For Anne's education, abruptly halted at the Grove School, Highgate in 1922, was now of some concern. Weekly lessons from the village school-mistress at Elworthy had not restored any sort of proficiency in French or mathematics.

At Stogumber they were briefly co-lodgers with the district nurse in an ancient thatched cottage. This proved too damp for AVS who 'had rheumatic fever, you know, when in Rome. I was quite given up – only brought round by a nun reading the Form for the Dying to be Received into the Roman Church'. They made their fourth move to another farm, Brewers Water, a stone's throw from Stogumber station.

Here, Anne fell ill again. The local doctor advised riding: 'And I mean proper disciplined riding, not tearing about on a pony'.

An introduction was made to a stable at Bicknoller. This was run by the ebullient Captain Evans Smith, who scratched a living by schooling polo-ponies and boarding horses too errant to be controlled by their owners.

At Brewers Water Anne began her journal. Her circle had not been large – the doctor and his wife, the district nurse, and a few local clergy. AVS' relatives came and went and there were the old friends at Elworthy. Among these, of the greatest interest to Anne, were the Sweet Escotts at Hartrow Manor. The Reverend Herbert had taken Anne riding, and besides, coached backward boys of whom several were of foreign extraction.

But now Captain Evans Smith and his wife, new surroundings, and friends made at school were enlarging Anne's life. She began to be interested in people as well as in the country and to face the days full of excitement. Feeling the urge to record all this, she began her diary.

CHAPTER I

April 23rd – May 29th, 1925

❧❀❀❁ ❀❁❀❀

A PRIL 23rd. The West Somerset Foxhounds Point-to-Point was held today and I went with the Sweet Escotts. I started off dressed in my new suit, though it was raining and AVS said "Take my advice and wear your old coat."

However, it cleared up before I reached the house.

I love going to Hartrow; after the long climb up Ashpier it is pleasant to go down the steep drive. Mr Sweet Escott says he can remember, as a boy, the chains still on the Scots fir where a man on the estate was hung at the time of the Monmouth Rebellion. He told me too that the Gothic Great Hall that makes a wing of the Georgian house is a modern sham.

He and I had an early lunch together. He doesn't look so much like the White Knight in his home as he does on a horse. More what he is, a venerable squire, with his white moustache and tweeds.

Penachi, the Greek boy, arrived late for lunch, resplendent in plus fours. He has beautiful manners. Mrs Sweet Escott and her sister hovered about. Then Mr Harry Sweet Escott arrived in his car; he and his father sat in front and Penachi and I squeezed into the dicky.

We talked about Russians chiefly; I told him about Miss Loris Melikoff at the Grove School at Highgate and how she escaped from the Bolsheviks across the frozen Finnish Gulf, pulling her aged mother on a sledge. He told me similar tales of Russians he knew.

The race-course was crowded, tipsters and bookies shouting and everyone buzzing with excitement. There was a smell of crushed grass and near the paddock, of horses. Mr Sweet Escott and I walked about; I recognised some of the throng and wondered who the large families of boys and girls might be. But there was a keen east wind and I was soon extremely cold. I longed for my warm old coat. Besides, I had to admit that my knitted coat and skirt looked wrong, everyone else being in brown tweeds.

Mr Sweet Escott would not bet without the advice of his son, so we had to find him before every race. I was thankful for the shelter from

3

the wind and the warmth of red-faced humanity as we lined up at the bookies. But the races were thrilling and nearly made me forget the cold. The last excited me most, as Captain Evans Smith was riding Filbert and Major Storey Skipper, both ponies I know. Filbert was last but one in starting, but gradually passed horse after horse and came in third. Skipper led the whole way round and won. He deserved to – he took the huge banks like a bird.

We did not stay to see the prizes given, for which I was thankful, being by then completely frozen. But tea at Hartrow thawed me and it was fun comparing notes. Penachi had lost on every race, Mr Sweet Escott won 5/- on Skipper and Harry was all square. So we did not do over well. I walked home; three miles.

April 24th. Captain Evans Smith told me about the race while saddling up before my ride today. Filbert would have done better if Michael Bucknell had not fallen under his nose at the first fence – the Captain had to rein up and so lost time. I had the honour of riding Filbert today. Paul the stable boy rode Mildmay, the pretty little liver-chestnut mare and led The Dun, and the Captain the brown Heatherbloom, leading naughty James Pigg.

We rode to Williton along lanes to St Audries, where the oaks are already coming out in the park, and down the long hill.

There were splendid views to Minehead and the sea; the sun was warm and the wind not so cold; big white clouds sailed the blue sky. All the meadows looked vividly green and were sprinkled with daisies and celandines. Everywhere the hedges were powdered with buds and gardens gay with wall-flowers and polyanthus.

This afternoon I went into the wood to pick violets and primroses. The wind filled the tree-tops with a rushing sound; they swayed against a blue sky. I sat on a log and watched and heard a chiff-chaff and thrushes singing.

Then I followed the brook; it curled and sang, with dimples and creases in the clear water. Along the banks were wood anemones.

> And lady-smocks all silver white
> And cuckoo-buds of yellow hue.

An ousel flew up the stream and three calves came up to me to stare. I picked whole sheaves of king-cups and some watercress, which was delicious for tea.

April 25th. AVS' Birthday. While Winter, the groom, was lunging the new colt today, it broke loose and galloped up the drive. The goats and their kid were terrified – the kid ran against the colt's legs but luckily was not hurt. The drive gate was shut for once and the colt wheeled and took a flying leap into Miss Richardson's garden,

4

scattering the poor lady and her gardener left and right.

When order was restored we rode up Bicknoller Combe, the Captain and Winter leading horses and I on Filbert. It was glorious on top, pleasantly fresh with a view of pale sea and a misty sky.

After a time Filbert grew restless – I was leading Heatherbloom about while the others were schooled and as I was riding with only a curb, I could not touch his mouth. Then I saw the reason – the hunt was below us in the Combe. I called the others and we departed by another route. On the way home I had a lesson on riding with a curb and on collecting a horse to get his hocks under. I like the Captain immensely.

I stayed to lunch; it was a hilarious meal as we had 'suety pud' and

James Pigg, the dog not the horse, adores it. He grew wildly excited and gulped down a plateful. We talked of the war and the prospect of another, and the Captain described in glowing terms how greasy, slimy rats ran over him in the trenches.

James Pigg

We had a sumptuous birthday tea-party for AVS – an iced cake with a huge candle stuck in the middle. Mrs Webb the doctor's wife came with her sister and Mollie, AVS' sister, who is staying with Nurse. She has a 'pash' on Mrs Webb; I am not surprised as she is a charming woman.

Mrs Webb sat on the sofa on which AVS was reclining – she has not been well – and talked to her.

April 26th. I walked to church at Stogumber this morning, and wrote a long letter to Mother, all about riding. I wonder what she thinks of it?

Mollie came to tea and talked a great deal of Christian Science. Of course, as Mrs Webb is a Scientist, Mollie is full of it – it would be just the same were she a Mormon! For some time there has been a great mystery, preserved by Mollie, about this, but yesterday the doctor told AVS quite openly about his wife's belief, which has put an end to rather an absurd state of affairs.

Mollie promised me a hat she does not want – a pretty brown straw one. She and I went out to watch motor-trials rushing up our hill. One of the cars was driven by William, an interesting figure to me as AVS says he has a bad reputation with girls. How can she know this? I am not allowed to know him, though his sister is approved of.

April 27th. I had to clean the rooms today so got up early and finished them before breakfast. Even so, I was late in arriving at Bicknoller where to my joy the Captain, Winter, and I rode out to a meadow for a gallop. They were on James Pigg and The Dun and I on Mildmay. Milly when roused is very fast indeed and The Dun a real racer, so it was great fun. We galloped four times round the field.

After lunch came the usual rush to get the Captain off to polo.

"Cecil, have you found your clean breeches?"

"Ducky, fly and get me my yellow sweater. – Oh damn, where the deuce did I put those confounded spurs?"

"Cecil, do hurry up, the car's waiting, you'll be late."

At last he left and we enjoyed a peaceful afternoon gardening.

The swallows have come at last. A pair was twittering and preening on a roof this morning. We have heard a cuckoo for some days now.

I will finish by saying that it is nine o'clock and the birds are still singing. The world is a deep ultramarine-indigo, looking out from our lamp-lit room. I like Daylight Saving!*

April 28th. I was trying to find a hammer down at the stables this afternoon when the colt broke away from its schooling in the paddock and galloped up the drive.

There came a yell – "Who the hell's left the bloody gate open?" and the colt tore off down the lane.

The sudden appearance of Mr Sweet Escott in the pony-trap stopped him, Hitchy Koo the Shetland bravely blocking the way. Paul had meanwhile saddled Milly and set off in pursuit, so quite a procession returned, Paul leading Milly, the Captain with the colt and Mr Sweet Escott in the trap drawn by valiant little Hitchy. He is a character, and achieved fame out hunting last winter by bucking David Holden straight into a holly bush.

Mr Sweet Escott was even more white-knightly than usual; one almost expected to see the pony-trap hung with bee-hives. He stayed gossiping for quite twenty minutes. His time being his own, the dear old man is oblivious of his victims' occupations.

April 29th. I went to Dunster today to watch the Indian team play polo, the Captain having kindly arranged it. My train got me there much too early, so I took a walk along the Minehead road. A car drew up and and young man offered me a lift, which I politely refused, having had many warnings from AVS on the subject. I found a good seat on return and watched people streaming in. At 2.45 the ponies

* Daylight Saving, a one-hour change in time, was introduced in Great Britain in 1916, as a war-time measure to save fuel.

6

paraded. First came a stately Indian bearing a flowing banner, followed by all the ponies, each led by an Indian groom. Then a gap, and then an English boy with a banner and our ponies and grooms. The English looked rather fed-up with parading and showing off, whereas the Indians revelled in it. Their ponies had bright ribbons and plaited martingales of ribbon and cord.

Just as play started, down came the rain, which was good for us, as we are used to it and they are not. Goals mounted up very evenly and we ended all square. I loved seeing the ponies galloping at full speed and the riders leaning over to take a steady shot that sent the ball spinning 100 yards. And it was fun too, to see the ponies crash into each other to prevent a shot.

In the tea interval Captain Evans Smith came and found me, got a table, and in a masterful way went off to the kitchen, returning with a good supply of cakes, bread and butter, and a huge teapot. We had a lovely tea together and I saw lots of people I knew.

Then I sat in the enclosure and watched another match; then said goodbye to the Captain, who gave me two badges for AVS and me to come tomorrow. I caught the train home; AVS came to meet me with an umbrella and said that Dr Webb will take us tomorrow. Hurray!

The rain has stained the new hat rather, I'm afraid.

May 4th. AVS' brother, Edward, has come to stay. He is decidedly not so nice as last time – he puts on so many airs with his swell plus fours. But he took AVS and me to Minehead today and stood us a beano lunch in the luxurious dining-room of the Plume of Feathers. We went out to Dunster but it was too wet for play so we returned for tea at the Beach Hotel. It was even grander than the Plume and we had the large drawing room all to ourselves. I began to think Edward nice after all.

May 5th. I said goodbye to Edward and set out for Bicknoller through showers. It became too wet to ride so I watched Captain Evans Smith schooling Watershed in the riding-school. It was interesting, as he explained it all as he went. Watershed hated 'passage' and it took a long time to get him to do it correctly. He was sworn at as punishment and rewarded by a pat and "Good boy".

A cuckoo flew past me, quite near, as I was sowing nasturtium seeds for Mrs Evans Smith.

May 6th. It is the first day of term and we are to do Keats for literature. Last term I said how much I should like to do modern verse and we did and now it is the same thing – almost uncanny.

Miss Briggs [the headmistress] gave out that she was taking all the girls to polo in the afternoon. I *was* envious!

When I got home AVS said ''Why not go on the 2.20 train and join them?'' – So I gobbled my lunch and changed in ten minutes, which must be a record.

The Indians were playing Cirencester; a very good match. I sat with the school and when I went to get my tea-ticket, the man could not change 2/6d. A very nice fair young man offered to help and gave me 1/6d. We haggled and haggled over the change; I grew thoroughly muddled and he fed-up. Eventually, he departed and I found 6d in coppers. It *was* absurd – and he was so nice.

The Rajah (Rao Rajah Hanout Singh I believe) played splendidly and we saw some brilliant play. I stayed for the second match as I wanted to see the Captain performing; I was glad I did for he played well.

May 7th. After tea I took the farm-dogs to the bluebell wood. They enjoyed chasing the young rabbits. It was showery, and bright sunshine made the wet leaves look verdant. Silver birches, oaks, and beeches were all in young leaf, while the bare trees were misted with crimson buds. The lanes were full of dog violets; I've never seen so many; in places the banks were blue with them.

The bluebells were just coming out in the copse, enough to throw a pale-blue mist over the carpet of dog-mercury and there were masses of crimson-purple orchids glowing against the green hazel bushes. In every tree birds were singing, while a cuckoo called from the spinney beyond. I walked home thinking all the time of Walter de la Mare.

May 11th. Mr Sweet Escott's hunter, Dander, has been very ill – is dead! I first heard of it from David, who came with his bicycle which the village taxi could not take up to Hartrow. It was their first day of term and David was returning from holidays.

''Is it true about Dander?'' he asked, having heard of it from the driver. I told him I didn't know.

Then yesterday at Bicknoller, Mrs Evans Smith said ''Isn't it terrible about Dander!'' She said the vet had to kill him as he was in such pain.

Later, when Dr Webb took us on his rounds and had gone into a cottage, David passed riding Peter, the Hartrow grey. I asked if Mr Sweet Escott was much upset and he said no, he didn't think so.

Guy Sadler [another boy at Hartrow] has just been in for David's bike, and told us that Dander died of lock-jaw, the result of an infected cut, and that the poor thing died before the vet got there. It is a dreadful story and I am grieved.

Guy is very keen on my going up to Hartrow for tennis of an evening. It is difficult to arrange, as some evenings he will be playing cricket at the Stogumber club and some I'll be staying for tennis at school and on others Mr Févre [the village schoolmaster] is giving him maths lessons.

May 14th. Mr and Mrs Chorley (he used to be vicar at Monksilver) took us out in their car this afternoon; we went to see the Cases at Brompton Ralph. Mrs Chorley advises her husband on his driving all the time; she and AVS sat in the back and she was constantly shouting "Horn, Falconer, horn!"* which rather disrupted conversation. We found Mr and Mrs Case at home. After tea they took us round the Rectory garden; it's a perfect dream of green leaves, flowers and smooth daisied turf. Mr Case told us about the church. He is having wonderful results both at Tolland and Brompton; people are beginning to come, even to early service.

On the way home, the Chorleys dropped in at Monksilver to see some of their old parishioners. There was just time for me to run up to the Rectory, which I did, though AVS was much against it. I thought she felt afraid I might keep the Chorleys waiting so I hurried. I found Mrs MacTaggart with Marjorie Case, who is staying there.

We went up to see the MacTaggart boys, just in bed. I went to Chrys first. "Hulloh, Chrys, do you know who I am?"

"Chrysie Darling, say 'How do you do' nicely", said his Mama.

"Silly chow-chow", shouted Chrys.

I turned my attention to Basil, who squirmed and giggled and shouted "Silly chow-chow."

"Basil, how can you be so rude?" said Marjorie, whereat they giggled the more.

I rushed back to the car to find AVS raging at my having gone at all. Matters were not improved by my omission to say that she had been ill and not able to get over to see them, or walk up from the car.

"Of course, Mrs MacTaggart knows I'm here," she said, very truly. I was most penitent, but did not see the use of weeping o'er spilt milk. AVS continued to reproach me bitterly and I was altogether thankful when the Chorleys at last appeared.

May 16th. I planned to go to Elworthy, but awoke to a thick fog. I did not really mind it but had a good old grumble and received a lecture, to which I retorted. The long and short of it was that I was

* Many years later a daughter of Anne's saw on a second-hand book-stall a paperback entitled *Safety First*, by Falconer Horn. Surely a *nom-de-plume* by someone who knew the old parson!

most disgracefully rude and AVS kept me in all the morning to do sewing and housework.

She let me start at noon. I got up to Elworthy and went to see Mrs Ware first. Then Mrs Stephens at the cottage, who with all the children has had measles. Her husband had to do all the work until Edith came from service; her mistress allowed her a month's holiday.

It was just like coming home to walk through the court yard at Whites Farm. The little gate banged behind me and my feet made the same sound over the cobbles. They were sheep-shearing under the apple trees in the orchard – it was by now grilling hot. Ned appeared from the granary, and Mrs Hayes from the porch and welcomed me in. Poor old Isaac was in the back'us nursing a sick headache. Presently Gordon came bouncing in, taller than ever and rosy as an apple.

The morning slipped by quickly listening to Mrs Hayes' gossip: "Let me see, when was it? 'Twere last year, no 1923, and the pigs were three days old. 'Twere the 9th of March then and Ned, 'e come in with a bloke who 'ad his brother's wife's leg knocked off in an accident the year before.'' She remembers everything in her life, dates and all.

We had a regular farmhouse dinner of salt boiled pork. The sheep-shearers, Frank Waterman and his tall handsome son, came in and ate a large quantity. Baker Jones dropped in with the bread, sat down and gossiped, just like old times. He thinks I have grown up far smarter than he'd have thought from a little 'un!

After dinner, Mrs Hayes asked me to go down to our old dining-room and help choose a wall-paper, as they are having the room re-decorated. They had selected the most ghastly dark brown one, with red cherries at intervals. I managed to persuade them against it and we finally chose a very pretty one. My good deed for the day. I then went down to the Middletons, but they were out.

May 18th. When I got back from school, on the later train because of tennis, I saw AVS peeping round a corner and wondered why she had come to meet me – and then I saw a tall figure in grey and it was Mother! I *was* surprised, just as the two old dears intended. They had been planning it for weeks.

After tea I took Mother out to try and hear what I think is a nightingale and, as we went through the thicket, we heard it, quite close. Mother says it certainly is a nightingale. It was very beautiful – such marvellous trills and runs, and then a single low note repeated several times as a prelude to a burst of passionate trills. We walked through the wood in Kensie Lane. The undergrowth has shot up and everything is hidden by fresh green leaves. Then we wandered up the meadows, following the brook, and came out into the little lane. It was peaceful; no sound but the birds' quiet joyful singing.

May 29th. I went to tea with the Middletons, it being Mr Middleton's birthday. I walked to Stogumber and got a car up Ashpier Hill and from there walked along the top road, down Whitstone Nap and across Ham, which is a sheet of buttercups. The Middletons have two darling hound puppies at walk, Spaniard and Singwell. I took an Eversharp pencil as a birthday present – a great success.

Mr Middleton drove me to the top of Ashpier, where we discovered Polly's near-hind shoe was nearly off. I stooped down in the mud and pulled and tugged, while Mr Middleton held her head. It was blowing hurricanes – pouring with rain and our hats kept careering away. I got covered with mud and cut my hand on Polly's shoe, so that gore and mud were mingled. Eventually, I got it off and we said goodbye. When I reached Stogumber garage a car was coming out; it was Mrs Rutt, who gave me lessons at Elworthy – she offered me a lift as far as the station, for which I was most grateful, being wet and still bleeding.

CHAPTER II

May 31st – July 23rd, 1925

✻✻✻✻✻ ✻✻✻✻✻

*M*AY 31st.   Dicky, my eldest brother, has come for the weekend on his motorbike, and has set up his tent in the meadow. AVS and I went to church at 8.0 a.m. and breakfasted with Nurse. Dear old Miss Hall, who also lodges there, spoke of her nephew, Andrew Cruikshank, of whom she is very fond. She hopes he will be coming to stay soon. She is rather concerned at his deciding to be an actor; apparently, he shows great talent. I do hope he will do well.*

Then Dicky and I went for a long walk to Heddon Oak, across the level crossing by the stream, and through woods in Sixty Acres and Rexton Gorse. The sun was sifting through the beech leaves and all manner of birds were singing.

After lunch we started for Elworthy. Dicky took me on his flapper-pillion; I didn't quite like going downhill, it seemed so easy to slip off.

The church bell was ringing and Isaac hobbling down the road when we arrived. Mrs Hayes and Gordon came running out, awfully pleased to see us. Ned was too; we sat and talked while they finished their dinner and then went round the yard to inspect the calves, etc. Also the re-decorated dining-room. It was absolutely ripping, though I say it as shouldn't, seeing I insisted on the papers.

Then Ned had to change and shave. He emerged looking most handsome and dapper from the back'us. Mrs Hayes and her sister-in-law laid a divine farmhouse tea. Three sorts of jam, a huge plate of thick slices of bread, generously spread with creamy home-made butter, a junket, large bowl of clotted cream and two sorts of cake. We all gathered round, Dicky and Gordon in the window-sill, Ned and I in the settle, Isaac and Mrs Welsh opposite the window and Mrs Hayes at the top to dispense the tea. It was jolly in the dear old kitchen with sides of bacon in the oak rack, the dark beams and little leaded panes

---

* He became a well-known actor; one of his best-known roles was in the long-running TV series *Dr Finlay's Casebook*. He has been associated with the Edinburgh Festival for a number of years.

in which flies buzzed. We all talked at once and laughed a lot.

Then we 'went round'. First to Copse Mead. Words won't tell how lovely it was – the grass vividly green and spangled with flowers, the spinney all in bright young leaf and above the tops of the trees Elworthy Combe rising up in great walls of bracken, the thorn trees like islands of deeper green. As we climbed the hill we looked into the bottom of the combe and saw it all misted with bluebells. Deep in the thick foliage wood pigeons cooed dreamily.

Ned lifted us poor weak females across the brook and we scrambled up the steepy field to Dark Lane, which we walked along and in across Five and Six Acres, where we admired the ewes and lambs. As we came out into Hill Road we saw 'old Georgy Norman' the horse-dealer, ambling down the steep hill, his grey pony shuffling behind. His long overcoat was in tatters about his calves, his battered bowler with its rim falling over his eyes, his boots unlaced and his trousers in fringes, with a dirty layer of skin between them and his boots. Why such a figure should be credited with vast riches is beyond me. When he mounted his saddle slipped round, the girths being slack, but after a few attempts he somehow got himself up and 'away du go,' his legs sticking straight out each side to match his elbows.

We drove the cows slowly home and then went to see Mrs Ware. Liza Grandfield was there, and we had a good chat. We heard again how the old sheep-dog had to be shut up for Farmer Ware's funeral but went straight to the grave when he was let out. He wouldn't leave and had to be shot. So poor Mrs Ware lost them both.

As we walked back for the motorbike, I told Dicky how Farmer Ware was to have taken me to the Peace Day Sports at Brompton in his dog-cart but AVS dreamt the night before that the horse shied and I was thrown out and killed. So she took me on the back of her bike. I was very disappointed but the colt did shy and Farmer Ware said he was glad I wasn't up in the high seat beside him.

June 1st.   I had asked Captain Evans Smith if Dicky might ride, so we went over quite early. Naughty James Pigg was being drenched [by having a bottle of tonic poured down his throat]; the Captain was apologetic about a mount, Heatherbloom being lame from a knock at polo, so Dicky had to ride Antics and we went to Elworthy Burrows instead of the Quantocks. The Captain rode Watershed, Winter The Dun and I had Mildmay.

The Dun has been entered for racing this season and it is hoped that she may win the Biddecombe Cup, with a prize of 200 guineas. She has the speed but will she use it?

The Captain and Dicky got on very well, as I had hoped. When we reached the jumping-fields on top of the Burrows, The Dun and

Watershed raced while we waited in another field. The Captain seemed quite pleased with The Dun's performance.

We rode back through Hartrow rookery and out by the back drive to Willet and Vexford and were dropped at Brewers Water. Dicky had thoroughly enjoyed it and said "You don't often meet such a nice chap", which I took as high praise. He packed up his tent and left for London directly after lunch.

June 5th. A red-letter day. I had sent a card to Captain Evans Smith, saying I would come over in quest of a ride. When I got to Bicknoller, I found Mrs Evans Smith tip-toeing about. It was grilling hot, and the Captain had a 'touch of the sun' and was lying down. We sat in the verandah and conversed in whispers; it felt as if there was a baby who must not be disturbed.

Eventually, he woke up and we had tea. He was evidently quite refreshed as he joked and told absurd yarns. We then went to the stables and he gave me a saddle and bridle saying "Let's see if you can saddle Mildmay yourself." So I went into her box and after a few shots got the bridle on. The saddle was easy. The Captain said one strap was wrong, so I altered it and then we rode to Woolston Moor. He put me back to very long stirrups; we cantered around, me trying hard to keep Milly balanced. But she was in a sloppy mood, making for the road whenever we were that side and stopping short when I turned her, so that I kept losing my stirrups. I did feel a fool!

The Captain came to my rescue; gave me his pony (the new one) to hold and proceeded to "wake Milly up!" He did wake her up too! He rode round and round kicking and swearing, till she thoroughly got the wind up. She then tore along, her head up and ears laid back, looking as spiteful as you please. When he got off she was streaming and panting. He was jolly hot too but still able to give her a good talking to. "You lazy sentimental, sloppy fool! You like hacking with ladies on you, don't you, and going into hedges to eat!"

After this, I managed her beautifully and she was as good as gold. I was pleased, as it was the first time I'd really succeeded, and I had a word of praise too, which pleased me more. Oh, it was hot! The ponies were soaked with sweat when we stopped and were sluiced down with a rag dipped in the stream. We led them home by the lanes, where gnats and mosquitoes did their gruesomest and horse-flies attacked the ponies. The Captain electrified me by saying "I may be able to give you some riding in September, Anne. I believe Dunster Show is in September; would you like to ride in the show-ring?" Oh, how lovely it would be!

When we got back, I looked at the stable-clock; to my horror it was 7.20. I had sworn to be home by 7.30, as Mrs Dark was giving us

14

cooked supper and it upsets her if I'm late. So when I said "My hat, it's 7.20," the Captain was dismayed and said "I'll ride you back." I knew he had four more ponies to school, so begged and implored him not to – he laughed and refused to let me walk. So Winter, the groom, rode me home as far as the turning down the lane and I ran the rest of the way. I was baking hot, and tired from legging up Milly, but kept on with clenched teeth and a pounding heart. I was so afraid AVS would say "No more riding"! But when I got in supper wasn't ready and there was time for a cool bath.

June 10th.   Friends of AVS, Dr & Mrs Wilkins, are again staying at Minehead, and offered to take us for a drive. So AVS came by train and met me at their hotel. Horner Woods were decided upon, which delighted me as I had not been there. It is a deep gorge winding between stupendous hills, one side wooded and the other bare, with rocks, bracken, and twisted thorns now white with blossom. Down the gorge tumbles Horner River, foaming between boulders and murmuring over speckled pebbles. There were clear pools fringed by ferns and waterfalls between mossy rocks.

The trees are very fine; huge oaks, hornbeams, and beeches; moss below them, here and there glades of soft grass. We had tea in such a place, and then Miss Neville, [a friend], the Doctor, and I wandered up the valley, leaving AVS and Mrs Wilkins to gossip.

We saw a huge buzzard float out to soar and sweep far above; it had a young rabbit in its talons. As the afternoon wore on the wooded side of the valley was bathed in brilliant light while the other was in deepest shadow. But in places the sun came through the woods we were in, lighting the green and dancing on the river.

We spent so long in this fairyland that we had a rush to catch our train. Mrs Wilkins was fearful of anything approaching fast driving and kept saying "A little slower, please!" as her husband chugged along. We were on tenterhooks the whole way – but we caught the train, just, and reached home safely.

June 12th.   AVS came with me to Bicknoller today for tea; Mrs Webb was there and drove her home. The talk was chiefly of her nephew, who is in the RAF; the Captain said that nothing less than £2,000 would induce him to fly and even then he would lie prone in the cock-pit!

He and I hacked to Williton for some errands, and had an interesting conversation chiefly about "these d– socialists"!

After a visit to the saddlers, we rode home and I heard about a favourite Irish terrier named Jorrocks. When stationed outside a town, the Captain often had to go on Parade and used to shut the dog up. But Jorrocks invariably escaped and learnt to take the tram to the

Barracks — he knew just where to jump on and off. The conductress often asked for a fare: "I'm sorry, Captain, but your dog had a ride yesterday. I'll have to charge you."

The Colonel adored Jorrocks, although he would not admit it, referring to "that damned dog"; of course, Jorrocks knew this and fawned upon him, lying at his feet and dribbling on his boots.

While the Captain was at the Front, Jorrocks got out one night and killed a chicken at a farm. He was found shot, stone dead, with the chicken in his mouth. Mrs Evans Smith was heart-broken and all the town and regiment furious.

She could not bear to write the news to France, so asked a brother officer on leave to break it. Her husband, meanwhile, was wondering why she never mentioned the dog in her letters. I gathered that even now one does not mention the tragedy in front of her.

I stayed to groom and water Mildmay, who, poor mare, has heat-bumps under her saddle, mowed the lawn and gave the garden a good drenching. It was nearly ten o'clock by the time I had walked home.

June 21st. I've long noticed from afar a very nice, good-looking youth of twenty-five years or so, who travels on my train each morning. I've always liked him because he fools with the schoolboys so rippingly and lets them cheek him. He wears immaculate plus fours and a pork-pie hat and is an architect – I know that, as he sometimes carries large rolls of mapping paper. His name is E. Browne – it's in Indian ink, in lovely neat printing, on his plan-book. All these interesting facts have been gathered sitting opposite to him.

On Thursday, I got into the train with him and a woman who also comes each day and with whom I often talk; she is clever and interesting [the manageress of a shop in Minehead]. This morning we began on the everlasting subject of the war and I aired my usual views that we should all be dead against another.

Miss Ford brought Mr Browne into the discussion by looking at him and saying "I believe men enjoy a good scrap sometimes." So then we all began upon this burning topic and upon Socialism, Germany, China, etc.

On my return, I got into a carriage containing two diminutive children. Just before the train moved off, E. Browne strolled up the platform, looked in and went on! In a minute he returned and got in. We began to talk and before long were deep in water-colours, the country and our common liking for *Lorna Doone,* which he has been reading in the train. I learnt from Miss Ford that his father is an architect and that he is delicate.

On Friday, much to my surprise, I had a letter from Rex, AVS' nephew, which quite put E. Browne out of my head. Rex has sent me a book called *The Week-End Book*. It is an anthology of verse of every kind, songs, (tunes and all) recipes, first-aid, and games to play, wet or fine. It is a perfect gem; I shall much enjoy showing it to Mr Browne.

June 24th. My school-friend, Keren Wood, came for tea today on the 4.45 train.* AVS cut lamb and tongue sandwiches, I got young lettuces from the garden and with our sketching things crammed into Keren's satchel we started out for a day on the Quantocks. We went up Crowcombe as it's cool there under the beeches and yews. It was very hot when we came out on top; so we made for Seven Wells Combe, where the rhododendrons were in full flower, alternating with glades where a few bluebells lingered. We sketched and found a cool spot for lunch on the banks of the brook.

Keren paddled and I dozed under an oak. Caterpillars let themselves down onto me by silk threads and wee beasties came out of the grass stems and twiddled their feelers at me. We attempted another sketch further on, where we looked into an oval meadow through a gap in the trees, high hills on either side. Then we packed up and began the walk home.

We climbed up the hill by a deer-track and came out on a bare moor where heather and whortleberries grew among rocks. It was cooler here, as a fresh breeze came from the sea, but too hazy to see far; we could just see the Channel shimmering in the heat.

After a good tramp through the heather, we came down by Halsway Combe, to be met at the gate by AVS with the news that it was 6.55 and Keren's train left in ten minutes! She gobbled down some supper and departed while I rested my weary limbs. By the map I think we must have walked about fifteen miles.

June 25th. I had a headache today, I feel sure the result of certain mathematical problems that Miss Webster gave us for homework. Last night I spent over an hour beaten by it, so I enlisted the aid of the Station Master, Mr Barnett, when he came for his milk. He has often found answers to my sums but was unable to solve this one. The illustrious Keren, bright star, was the only one in our class to get it right.[†]

The headache was so bad that I abandoned my prep. this evening and went for a stroll.

* The last of a long line of Keren Woods. See Kilvert's Diary: 'Sweet Keren Wood' and 'Keren Wood's Wedding'.

[†] About sixty years later, she said only because her father had worked it out.

For the first time I realised that summer is here. Full-blown roses, wreaths of honeysuckle and white elderflowers were in the hedges and moondaisies in the long hay grass. By the brook the rising meadow made a green cup, and the stream sang to the grasses hanging over it. From a wild-rose bush petals fell and drifted down the water. I like to think it will always be the same for me to return and find nothing changed.

June 26th.   Haymaking has been going on and today the hay at the stables was carried, the waggons with their great horses lumbering up and down the drive. Winter and Paul were making the rick and the Captain schooling a new brown colt – a real beauty. They were all too busy to give me a ride so I did some gardening.

At tea, which the Captain and I took together, I was told a great deal about the colts and especially about The Dun. She is a real problem and is wearing the Captain out. He spent seven hours on the hills recently, trying to get her to go forward – she pranced and danced the whole time. At last he threw her and sat on her head! He tried her bare-back and she stood straight up on her hind legs, with him hanging on for dear life round her neck. And he has never seen such a kicker; she has been on the sick-list lately as she kicked herself under the heart. It is a thousand pities, as she could be such a lovely racer. We think she must be a mental case.

June 28th.   Dr and Mrs Webb took us on the rounds today. The Doctor wanted his wife to drive so he and I sat in the dicky. We met the Hartrow turn-out just in the narrowest part of the lane. Archer driving with Magnus the Swedish boy. We went to Preston, then to a cottage near Rexton Gorse, then to Rexton where we saw Ned's sister, Annie Chidgey and her daughter Dolly. On to the turn-pike at Holy Thorn, which Ned says was planted by Joseph of Arimathea on his way to Glastonbury.

We saw a most extraordinary sight in a field at the top of the Vellow Lane: a large flock of magpies, apparently holding a parliament. I counted twenty-seven. We then went by a charming lane at the side of Combe Wood; it was so shady and peaceful that we stopped and sat awhile.

When we moved on it was discovered that we had a puncture. Mrs Webb mended it, as she wanted to learn how. We came home through Lydeard St Lawrence, passing Baker Pullen's shop, and Crowcombe Heathfield.

July 3rd.   I had not seen Mr Browne for two days but travelled with him today. We had a heated argument over the merits of our newspapers. He takes the *Morning Post* and the *Times;* we agreed that any paper is better than the *Mail*.

I found the stables deserted in the afternoon, save for Paul, who told me I was to take Milly to Woolston Moor, where I should find the Captain. I met him on the way and he said I must take myself off alone. Feeling rather proud at this, I rode past Wexacombe and up on the Quantocks.

Milly was sluggish and would try to eat from the hedges; I felt ashamed when we passed people.

However, once on the hills she behaved better. One could see every detail of the Welsh coast and each bush and tree on Exmoor and the Brendons. The sea was blue with violet streaks. Wales was blue with shining cliffs and towns and a long streak of gold marking the coast. Exmoor purple-blue, and between stretched the valley, nine miles of chequered fields – red, yellow, green, darker woods and roofs half covered in trees.

All the time cloud shadows raced over, changing the colours from sunny yellow-green to deepest purple. I could see the white tents of the Doniford Camp and the guns lined up on the cliffs. An aeroplane was humming over our heads; however, it didn't come very near.

When we reached the top of Staple Hill we felt the full force of the breeze straight from the sea. The tops of the young bracken fronds bent down and let it skim over their heads. Away in the valley it was rippling the young corn; out to sea white horses were prancing on the waves.

I rode home by Bicknoller Post. It was strange suddenly dropping down to the shelter of the combe, away from the wind and broad expanse.

July 5th. We went out with the Webbs again today. Mrs Webb drove, so once again the Doctor and I sat in the dicky. He was in one of his playful moods and kept pinching me, but he was most entertaining. We drove round Tolland; church was just over and we passed Mrs Case and Marjorie, and Mrs Middleton walking home in a bright cotton frock.

Coming home Mrs Webb and I sat together and talked of music and poetry – and then of death.

July 7th. Today I witnessed The Dun's behaviour with my own eyes. The Captain rode her over to fetch me, with Winter on the new brown, leading Jessie for me.

We rode up behind Halsway Manor and The Dun was hopeless. Halfway up the Captain had to get off; he strapped up her near-fore and sat down to wait until she could behave herself. Winter and I rode

19

on, his comment being "Which of them will get tired first?".

It was a nice ride, along the top to Bicknoller Combe, but it began to rain as we neared home – a thundery day.

Mrs Evans Smith and I had our tea; the Captain didn't come and didn't come. We grew quite worried, knowing what a brute The Dun can be and how she kicks.

At half past eight, they returned, exhausted, and The Dun limping from kicking herself. Needless to say, all thoughts of racing her have been abandoned.

July 9th. Last night there was a search-light display. It is quite extraordinary how the camp at Doniford has spread. The country abounds in abominations such as telegraph wires along the lanes, search-lights on the hills, trolleys and cars everywhere and soldiers billeted in all the inns.

When I was in bed an aeroplance came humming along and suddenly the sky was alive with giant beams of light – broad swords – and then I saw the plane, just like a golden bee. It reminded me of the zeppelin at Highgate that was shot down at Potters Bar; I thought I had forgotten all about it but remembered it lit up by searchlights just like this. Every now and then the guns at Watchet fired.

Presently the vixen who has her cubs behind our pig styes came along and started yapping. The farm dogs woke up and barked and this aroused the ducks, hens, and geese who all joined in. Altogether a lively night.

July 11th. Today some fan-tailed pigeons arrived by rail from a cousin of Miss Hall's. She is giving them to me and I to the Sweet Escotts as their dove-cote has been empty for years. So in the afternoon we chartered a car and drove to Hartrow with the basket.

Mrs Sweet Escott, Archer and the Swede, Magnus, were there alone, David having been dragged off by Mr Sweet Escott to see a cricket match between Stogumber and Williton, in which Guy was playing. Archer, Magnus, and I put the pigeons in the dove-cote. Mrs Sweet Escott seemed delighted to see the old cote tenanted again.

After tea AVS and I walked down to Elworthy where the Hayses and Mrs Ware were overjoyed to see us. We went back to Hartrow for dinner – to which Mr Sweet Escott and David arrived – and then the boys and I walked round the rookery and fields in quest of a rabbit. Archer has a new gun, a beauty with two barrels. It takes to pieces before you can say twink.

The car came for us at nine o'clock – it was a lovely drive home, lit by the low sun. The Quantocks before us were bathed in rich light, the combes in purple shadow.

Anne

Dicky. p.12, etc.

Mother and Rayne. p.26

Uncle Arthur. p.28, etc.

Father. p.35, 'an eminently
  respectable lawyer'

Isaac Hayes. p.56 'I used to have such good times with him'

Helen Marsden, p.26 'my school friend at the Grove'

Patty. p.90 'Narney under a large blue hat'

Joan Davy, p.44 'her education finished'

AVS

Ned, Maggie, and Gordon Hayes.
p.10, etc.

Mr Middleton, p.11, with
hound puppies at walk

Mr Wood, Keren's father. p.17, etc.

p.46, Mr and Mrs Sangar and Miss Smythe at Shirley

Mrs Evans Smith, p.50, with Gallant and Garter

Meet at Hartrow Manor. p.3, etc.

Polo. p.93 etc., Dudley Frost, Captain Evans Smith, Major Storey, Major Crosby

Opening meet of Devon and Somerset Staghounds at Cloutsham

Polo. pp.6,7, the Indian team

*p.32, Mrs Parkinson's picnic. Anne 3rd from right,
Helen 2nd from left*

p.18, Dr and Mrs Webb, with Anne in the dicky

Captain Evans Smith. p.4, etc.

Miss Webster. p.21, etc.

Anne sketching

Horner Woods, p.1

In the Brendon Hills

*Aunt Olive, Anne, and Father, p.37, at Stanton
St Gabriel*

Symondsbury, p.34 'lay just beneath us'

SYMONDSBURY

Morcombelake (No. 1)

Chap.3 Morcombelake and Hardown Hill
p.36. Lyme Regis

July 15th.   I lunched with the Woods today at Minehead. They were as jolly as usual and said they now regarded me as a regular guest, in token of which they had saved my napkin with its ring. So I felt one of the family.

Miss Hammet our painting teacher joined us, and with our tea and sketching things we toiled up North Hill until we came out through a fir plantation. I felt queer on Camp Hill; I hadn't been there since I was at St Aldwyn's School when I was eight years old, except in dreams. I remembered it, and the ghosts of little girls and myself in a funny brown knitted coat and black beaver hat with cherries round it seemed to be there, giggling and whispering.

On North Hill

Keren took us to a good place to sketch where the pinewood begins and a path leads to the view, framed by branches. We worked for an hour and then had tea. It was twilight and stuffy under the pines so we took our cups and buns and ran into the sunlight.

While I was saying goodbye to the Woods, Miss Webster, our English mistress, came in, resplendent in a new coat, pink dress, and a string of pearls. She has creamy skin with dark eyes, beautiful brows and masses of black hair.

She and Keren came to the station obstensibly to see Mr Browne, but he must have caught an earlier train. I felt proud to be walking with such a beautiful woman.

July 16th.   Today, travelling back, Mr Browne showed me a book of plans and photos of houses being built in garden cities. I recognised some at Welwyn which I saw when I stayed with Rayne.

Mr Browne asked if I kept a diary. I was startled; he asked it so suddenly; and replied "Oh, occasionally," whereupon he laughed. Somehow I felt ashamed at keeping this one – writing all about myself. However, as I like myself best, it is after all, natural! Mr Browne said he kept one. He loved *Reynard the Fox* which I lent him. He said that older people might be right and young ones bound to go wrong, because they act on impulse and have no experience. I thought of Rex and how he always says that 'age is unnecessary'. I'm glad to say that I do reverence old people and I like Mr Browne for it. I think the young are terrible nowadays to scoff at the aged.

21

July 17. I lost myself on the hills today, riding Mildmay. I must have taken the wrong path at Bicknoller Post, for it led me to a small combe with an avenue of beeches, with a splintered log across a gateway. I did not recognise this at all from the time I rode to Kilve in the winter.

I should have turned back had Milly not been so naughty; she wanted to keep turning herself. I knew I must not give in to her and kept doggedly on. At length I came to the edge of a large wooded combe running up into the heart of the hills. A track ran up it with some tents pitched at the side. I rode along the top; it seemed as if I could drop a pebble onto the tiny tents and trees no bigger than tufts of wool on a blanket.

I did not know where we were and had been told that Milly is to play polo tomorrow so was not to go too far or too fast. Presently, my little track dwindled away and I was left alone, alone, all all alone on a vast expanse of heather and gorse. I would have given pounds to see Bicknoller Post and had visions of arriving home hours late to find an annoyed Captain awaiting explanations. The knowledge that he is always so kind made it worse.

At long last – after what seemed hours in the heather – I sighted the path we had come on and once on that I trotted on, soon reaching the Post. Every turn now brought us visibly nearer home and when we arrived the Captain hadn't got back and his wife was not even aware that we were late.

July 18th. Miss Webster and Keren came for the day by the 12 o'clock train. We had an early lunch and then set out for the Quantocks. Talking the whole way, we climbed Bicknoller Combe, telling ghost-stories and recounting dreams and mysterious psychic happenings.

I told them how Olga Handyside met the Headless Horseman at Combe Sydenham. It was in daylight and she was riding up the lane that comes out at the top of Ashpier, known to be haunted. The lane curves and the hedges had been cut; she distinctly saw a tall black horse coming down the hill, its rider *without a head*. Her mare took fright at the same instant and bolted nearly all the way to Truckwell.

There seems no rational explanation for this, horse and rider were unfamiliar and assuming that whoever it was rode with his head sunk in his chest, why should the mare have been so alarmed? We wonder if the Sydenham family had a beheaded member.

A pause at the top of the combe to eat whortleberries led to talking of love; the most interesting subject of all. Miss Webster has been engaged for over a year to a young man in Ulster. Devoted to him as she is, she has her other romances – not at all surprising, seeing her attractions. She related some of these to our eager ears; an amusing one explained a sumptuous Christmas card she had, with a neat little sketch of her portmanteau, its label bearing her name and address. There was no signature, just 'from –, Wigan to Crewe' written under the sketch. She then remembered sitting opposite a young man in the train. They did not speak but when he got out at Crewe she caught sight of him on a distant platform and he smiled, lifted his hat, and waved goodbye. How did he know that she was 'Miss'? He must have noticed her engagement ring; a very observant young man.

After we had turned for home, it was discovered that Miss Webster's camera was missing, a small one given her by her fiancé. We turned back, all very miserable and determined not to leave the hills until we found it. And find it we did; Keren walked straight to the spot and picked it up.

How we talked all that afternoon! There were so many experiences to share, hopes to be compared and thrills to relate.

We had a merry supper back at Brewers Water, and then I went with them to the station, where we waited half an hour for their train. It steamed in at last and waving and smiling they were borne away.

July 19th. Four of the Hartrow boys came to tea today. I heard a great noise and went out to see what it was. An ancient equipage was drawing up in the yard, with an equally ancient horse in the shafts. The whole thing was swarming with boys, some on the shafts and one on the steed. It was the Hartrow dog cart, built in the year dot and divested of all its paint. Lacking a back seat, the boys had to sit on the floor with a cushion.

The steed was the mare I learnt to ride on; she seemed huge and gaunt after the polo ponies. The boys were David, Thompson, Archer, and Magnus. Davis unharnessed the mare and put her in the stable and they all trooped in for tea.

There were not enough chairs, so the armchairs were pulled up to the table. They all ate an immense amount; we talked an even greater and laughed even more.

After tea we wandered through the wood, and returned to tell ghost stories and play the confession game in the *Week-End Book*. When they left it was alarming to see the creaking dog cart rattling down the hill, piled high with boys clutching each other at every lurch and pursued by an irate Thompson who had somehow been left behind.

AVS and I then walked to Bicknoller with a rabbit for the Evans Smiths. We were caught in a heavy storm and took shelter in the New Inn.

23

We found Mrs Evans Smith curling her hair, preparatory to going out to dinner. Presently a voice was heard:

"Ducky, will you get my studs – they're in the bathroom."

"Poor Cecil," exclaimed his spouse, "he's caught like a rat in a trap. He's changing his clothes and there is no way out of the bedroom except through here."

July 23rd. I had made up my mind not to look out for Mr Browne today but when the train came in it was packed and I saw him in one of the few empty carriages. I must say my conscience pricked me when I saw Miss Ford in an equally empty one. Immodesty triumphed and I travelled with Mr Browne. He did look rather amused. Never mind, the term is over and I am going to my parents in Dorset on Saturday. Next term I shan't be so silly.

Our talk was interesting, but at Watchet a lot of little boys got in, most riotous; they kept us laughing at their pranks; when they grew too noisy Mr Browne quelled them with terrific frowns and at last took them up by their shoulders and planted them down on the seat like so many turnips. The most uproarious he kept out in the corridor by putting one foot against the door-handle. I like him more and more.

CHAPTER III

July 25th – August 29th, 1925

>✝❀ ❀✝✦

JULY 25th. The day of my journey to Morecombelake. We rose and caught the 8.10 to Taunton. A taxi took us to the market-place, where AVS saw me into the Chard 'bus, my box hoisted onto the roof. At Chard I changed into the Axminster 'bus, and at Axminster found that a Greyhound coach left for Bridport in 20 minutes. So I took that and reached Morecombelake an hour earlier than expected.

Having toiled up the hill to Hardown I, of course, found that Mother had gone to Axminster to meet me. Father had done his utmost to dissuade her, knowing we would miss one another. Hardown is just the same, the garden and the view perfect; the earth-closet still outside the back door.

We are a small party as yet but even so fill the house. A Mrs Cornish is cook and maid combined; she has a pretty little girl of seven, Audrey. I am sharing Mother's room but shall move into the dressing-room soon so that she will not wake me at five. She makes tea at that hour and begins work – she is writing a book about her cousin Samuel Butler.*

July 30th. I have developed a craze for gardening† and spend the evenings clearing brambles. Yesterday I cleared and cleaned the greenhouse. Father and I have a good walk each morning. I have not bathed yet – the weather is bad. We are expecting a young married couple, the Bedingfields, tomorrow.

July 31st. When our guests arrived, (by car), little Audrey, Mother and I were cutting the bushes round the cottage, buried in a jungle from which we had to hew our way for the necessary greetings. Denise Bedingfield is tall, with smooth black hair, worn shingled and with a

---

* *Samuel Butler and his Family Relations*

† It lasted all Anne's life

fringe nearly down to her eyes. Her eyes are immense with drooping lids and enormously long lashes. She has a sweet low voice, pleasant to listen to. She wears long strings of beads; Father says she is the sort of woman one never sees 'unadorned'.

Her husband is an artist, and her opposite in every way. His great forte is the anatomy of animals though I believe that he paints, draws and sculpts anything.

August 1st. Father, the Beding-fields, Audrey and I all walked to the sea, scrambling down the ravine at Stanton St Gabriel. I was interested in Mr Bedingfield; he talks well. From superstition, we got into religion; I was surprised to find him deeply religious. Mother being an atheist and Father practically an agnostic, I expected their friends to be one or the other. It was glorious on the beach, the sea deep blue, with green hollows under the waves. Audrey and I paddled; she was scared by the rough sea but soon enjoyed my jumping her over the waves and I enjoyed her laughter and little warm body close to mine.

Mother gardening in her oldest clothes

August 4th. We expected Cousin Harry Butler, from Bournemouth, to lunch. He was coming to help Mother with her researches. He arrived at 11 a.m., which was a shock. The drawing-room was in a mess with the flowers half dead and Mother was in the kitchen-garden picking peas. I rushed to fetch her and she came up hot and breathless, in her oldest clothes and army boots. She entertained Cousin Harry in the garden while I did the flowers and tidied up.

Meanwhile, time wore on and no meat arrived – and there were seven for lunch. Also there was no bread. Fortunately, Mrs Cornish is a woman who can see the humorous side of things, so instead of a wailing and a fluster in the kitchen, she sat quietly shelling peas and chuckling. Fortunately, butcher and baker came just in time and lunch was a success.

During all this a telegram arrived to say that Rayne has another son. We are all sorry it is not a girl this time. And after lunch, Margaret

Macgregor came up, to ask me if I would go to Charmouth to bathe with her. So I collected some tea and met her at the Ship Inn, where we caught a 'bus.

The beach was so crowded that we had to undress in a hut, for which hardship an old salt charged us 1/-. The bathe was worth it, the sea calm and warm. Margaret is a very pretty girl with short, fuzzy hair; she goes to St George's Co-Educational School near London.

We had to wait half an hour for a 'bus home, and I found the family at supper. Mother said "Of course, you haven't heard the family disaster, have you?"

My thoughts flew to another telegram announcing the death of the baby, or Rayne, or both, but it was only to say that 26 West Hill has been burgled. Having been assured that the books were safe, I felt quite happy. It is arranged that Mother will go to town tomorrow to see about it and return next day.

August 6th.   I awoke to hear low growls of thunder and rain pouring down. Denise is terrified of thunder and was prowling round the drawing-room looking thoroughly miserable. I did what I could to console her and drew the curtains. We lit the fire and spent a cosy morning in its warmth. After lunch 'Bear', as we now all call Mr Bedingfield, and I went in his car to meet Mother.

The burglary was very small – just the plated things not put in the bank, but every drawer in the house had been opened and the contents scattered about.

After supper the clouds rolled away, so we all went for a walk, except Mother, who prefers gardening. There is an attractive larch-wood on a steep hill in Marshwood Vale that I wanted to see, so we walked across a meadow to it. We found it surrounded by a deep ditch piled with thorns; Father and Denise sat on a mossy bank under an oak while Bear and I scrambled through into the wood. A path led round it; I had a mad fit and went bounding along, the rain-drops soaking my stockings and dress. The Bear followed more slowly, evidently fearing I had gone stark, staring mad. I was wringing wet when we left the wood, but dried as we walked home; Bear and I in front, walking ahead to keep warm as the others were so slow. We fell into our usual discussion on theology.

Denise had a talk to me when we reached home. She asked if I didn't think Bear the dearest little man in the world? She seemed very sad and told me that she has been ill (I gather from Father that she nearly smoked herself to death) and had a horribly sad childhood. In fact, the five years of marriage have been her only happy ones. Even then she lost both her babies, and has been very ill.

Poor things! They are a hopeless pair – quite lacking in common sense. Denise is always thinking of tragedy and has a pessimistic nature. She does not admit of a God and is afraid that evil may conquer good.

August 7th. The Bedingfield's last day. It was foggy and cold; Father asked for a fire in his cottage study so I lit it. The Bear insisted on coming with me to the village shop and back again for things I'd forgotten, and helped me pick vegetables. I wonder if he is so helpful in his own abode? After lunch, when I went out to the garden to finish my sketch he came too, hung over me and made suggestions which, as he is an artist, I felt bound to carry out. But it made rather a mess.

After an early tea, we all went in their car to the landslip between Lyme Regis and Seaton. Denise was terrified at the steep hills and I must say I felt uneasy, as the car is a 12 HP Morris Cowley and they had not tried her on bad hills before. We crawled up and down, shrieking loudly in bottom gear.

The car was left down a lane and we bought tickets for the landslip at a fine old farmhouse with mullioned windows and grimacing gargoyles. A short walk led to where the cliffs are slowly sliding into the sea. They go in great parallel ridges, with chasms between where the earth has cracked and gaped. These are full of fine trees, shrubs and ferns and flowers. Immense chalk bluffs, dazzling white, stand out from all this verdure and below, beyond the chaos of bluff and chasm, one sees the sea breaking on the rocky coast.

When we got home we found that Uncle Arthur, Father's younger brother, had arrived. He is the very peach of men – everyone loves him. He is 'long and lank and ribbed like the seasand' with grey curly hair, grey merry eyes and the most beautiful mouth. He is as brown as old mahogany and wears home-knitted khaki jerseys – never a collar and tie – and coarse flapping trousers and has an odd shambling gait that gets him along at surprising speed. He takes a long long time to speak as he stammers before a word, then a rush of words and then, again, that pitiful pause. And he tips his nieces and nephews 10/- and has everything one could possible want in his pockets and can turn his hand to anything, from cooking trout (having caught them) in brown paper over a camp fire, to mending a window-sash.

He plays Bridge with great skill and writes so well that one feels it a loss to the world that he has not written a book. He is a good shot too and knows England like a map – all the best routes and inns. He has friends all over the world and writes them long, charming letters, and writes, too, articles for various papers on strange plants, trees, pests, and agriculture. Such is our dear, humorous, odd, shambling, and utterly charming uncle.

28

We played Bridge after supper – Uncle and I versus the Bedingfields. They won – I am not good at Bridge – yet.

August 10th. Helen Marsden, my school friend at the Grove, Highgate, came to stay today for a fortnight. She has grown; is now 5ft. 6 inches with pink skin, hazel eyes and curly chestnut shingled hair, which shows off her beautiful neck.

A letter came from the Bedingfields, saying how much they enjoyed our society and learned talk. "No artist", added Bear "could fail to find inspiration amid those noble hills." Also "And Anne! Oh, how we did enjoy Anne, her freshness and naturalness, and her cleverness too!" My word, they do pile on the butter!

August 13th. A misty morning but it cleared in time for the fête at Whitchurch Canonicorum. Helen and I went down about 4.30 and found a watery sun shining on various stalls and tents. We were immediately pounced upon by a lady at the Lucky Dip and, having tendered 1/-, I found I had won a photograph of Madox Brown's picture of the emigrants. It seemed so quaint to find this old friend; we have it in the West Hill dining room; at a village fête. After this we listened to a performance on hand-bells; they sounded sweet and mellow in the open air.

We had tea in the village school-room and then Mother, Father, and Uncle Arthur arrived. We met Margaret MacGregor and skittled for a goose. I retired after knocking down one skittle.

The Bridport Band then marched round the field, followed by numerous youths in fancy dress, everything from a crinoline to a baby's long robe. Thus attired they proceeded to play football, most amusing to watch. We left about seven, quite tired.

August 15th. Margaret suddenly appeared after lunch, to say that Mrs Tolley, who had the Produce Stall at the fête, was giving a small impromptu dance this evening and would we go!

It sounded nice so we said we would, though we know nothing of Mrs Tolley beyond that she lives in a thatched cottage on the Whitchurch lane and that her husband is a fat major to whom we pay 3/- per year for dumping the contents of our Elsan on his common land, he being the Lord of the Manor.

We were much excited and spent no little time in polishing our shoes and deciding what to wear.

We found the company assembled on a paved terrace, reached by a flight of stone steps. Our host and hostess didn't seem to be present but we remembered that Margaret had pointed out a girl at the fête as Summer Tolley. So we marched up to her and said who we were. We talked to her till Major Tolley arrived and introduced us to the other guests.

The terrace had brick pillars at the end supporting a garden-room, and a low wall just right to sit on. A curved flight of steps led down to lawns and a tennis court, behind which were the beginnings of the house they were building when the war came. At the back of the terrace was a pool into which water splashed. And all around were strings of fairy lights which, as the sunset waned, began to glimmer like glow-worms.

Mrs Tolley arrived and put on the gramaphone and I was asked to dance by the elder son, a redhaired boy of about eighteen. There were about thirty people there, most of whom I knew by sight. The Lees came; Mr Lee is vicar at Whitchurch. Edward had grown since the donkey-cart days of five years ago; he is now tall, curly-haired and good-looking in an English way, Captain of the Whitchurch II and at Sherborne.

It was fun when it grew really dark and the lights shone from inky and mysterious shadows. They gave us supper in the garden room; coffee, lemonade, heaps of sandwiches, and fruit salad with clotted cream.

I danced every dance; two with Helen and with Mrs Tolley and Summer, who reminds me of brown sugar – moist and sweet. Then I danced with a nice little boy who enjoyed hearing about Archer's gun, and I had a very nice dance with a good looking sunburnt man with dark hair. He is an architect named Bob Coombes and such a jolly fellow. Helen liked him awfully. He came and held out his arms to me, to ask me to dance; I got up and he exclaimed "Heavens, we've not been introduced!"

The next dance he did exactly the same thing to Helen and told her: "I've just done an awful thing – held out my arms to a lady who flew into them, and I discovered we didn't know each other!"

I had two dances with Edward Lee. For the second we sat on the steps and he told me how he hopes to get into the Navy.

The time simply flew, till we had Auld Lang Syne, and Mrs Tolley rushed round with sparklers, shaking them over us till we were enveloped in fiery stars. Then we took our leave – it was the nicest dance I've ever been to.

August 19th. Aunt Olive Garnett has arrived and has Father's room; he is sleeping at the cottage. He asked me if I would like to earn some money. I said *"Rather"*, whereupon he gave me a beautiful etching of Fechter as Monte Christo, and asked me to copy it. He might as well have asked me to copy a Turner, but it was fun to do and the result not too bad if not compared with the original. He was pleased with my effort and gave me 4/-.

Believe it or not, Margaret again appeared to ask us to another dance! This is to be given by a Miss Williams, who lives at Whitchurch. I can't place her but Margaret says she was at the Tolleys.

In the afternoon, Uncle Arthur took Helen and me to Charmouth. The beach was crowded so we walked back to the village, "Had tea and then bus–t" as Helen put it. We then spent some hours beautifying ourselves, and called for Margaret. We had to go with her as we had no idea where Miss Williams' house, called Plenty, might be.

We walked and walked and *walked* and at last arrived – the house is miles beyond Whitchurch.

People were gathered on the lawn in fancy dress, chiefly as gypsies, and a lady was playing a squeaky fiddle. I recognised our hostess even though she was disguised in a Kate Greenaway cap, fichu and apron. We did country dances which none of us knew well; the result was an awful muddle.

The Tolleys arrived late, Basil in a huge apron, farmer's hat and a moustache suggestive of burnt cork. John was in his shirt-sleeves and Summer looked moister and sweeter than ever under an enormous sun-bonnet. Mrs Tolley was even more dashingly attractive in a scarlet hat with blue feathers at a rakish angle.

Country dances seemed rather flat after those at the Tolleys and Helen and I longed for proper dancing. Stumbling through 'Black Nag' into females yelling "Set and turn single", and having to hum the tune when the violinist ceased to play from sheer exhaustion, was rather too like school.

We had quite a decent supper, however, indoors, and then played games in the drawing room. I enjoyed one, at which the dark architect who is Miss Williams' nephew, presided over a blackboard. On this we had to draw in coloured chalks the event or famous character we had been given on slips of paper. Edward Lee did a very spirited one of Henry VIII, I had Lloyd George and Helen George V.

There was much merriment as we each paraded round the room with the board; some were exceedingly hard to guess. At this point Helen's nose suddenly bled; she constantly suffers from this; and she was ushered from the room by a motherly woman next to her.

We took leave at last and walked home with the exhausted violinist and two others. After we had left them and deposited Margaret at her gate, Helen, who had been mysteriously pinching my arm for some time, confided that she has fallen deeply in love with Bob Coombes, the architect.

I sympathise; he is awfully nice and good-looking, but

31

remembering Mr Browne (and try as I will, I can't forget him) I am not stricken with such pangs myself.

August 21st. Uncle Arthur suggested our all going to a cricket match at Bridport, so after bustling through some housework, we caught the 'bus. Mother came too, as she had some shopping to do. We had some difficulty in finding the ground, which is hidden behind a brewery a long way down the West Bay road.

The 'bus

Dorset were playing Wiltshire: and we saw some very good play, Wilts being dismissed for 75. Lunch-time came soon and we were just about to begin our weary trudge into the town when a dear old bean with a car of 1900 vintage kindly gave us a lift.

On our return, Dorset was in and made 150 runs before heavy rain stopped play.

I had a headache and was tired that evening so was not in the best of moods for an argument on hunting at supper. Mother moralised in her usual lofty vein and Aunt Olive in her brusque one. She sweeps away everything not belonging to her taste, never forgetting for one moment that she is the eldest daughter of the late Dr Richard Garnett, CB, LL.D, Keeper of Printed Books, etc. Rather rudely, I stuck up for sport, and Uncle Arthur stuck up for me. "Well, I tell you what," he said, "people who sit at home and eat mutton and beef had much better not abuse people who kill stags and foxes." I was grateful.

August 23rd. A stormy day made Helen and me anxious for a picnic to which a Mrs Parkinson had invited us, at Seatown.

It came on to pour as we walked there but we sheltered under a hedge and reached the beach fairly dry. Three girls who were at the Tolleys were there; Mr & Mrs Parkinson and his old mother, Bob Coombes (much to Helen's relief) and his father and aunt, Margaret and her mother and several more.

We arrived in time for an excellent tea, eaten squatting on mackintoshes around the door of the Parkinsons' hut. Then we amused ourselves by throwing ducks and drakes. Bob did it beautifully; his pebbles skipped and bounded for yards. Then he, Muriel, Margaret, Helen and I bathed. It was very rough; the enormous waves knocked us down when we tried to stand so we lay in the surf.

I felt brave and rather scornful of the others on the brink, so fought my way out to swim beyond the breaking crests. Just as I was serenely floating a huge wave came unawares and washed me under. There was a terrible roaring in my ears and the weight of tons of water; my head felt as if it were bursting blood.

I struggled to stand up and found I was out of my depth; there was just time to shout "Help!" before I went down like a stone. The awful roaring closed in like a thousand lions and I thought I had drowned.

Once again I came up and somehow Bob appeared and hauled me out. I scrambled through the surf more dead than alive and very sick. Bob looked scared and told me that the big wave had sucked me right out, over a deep pebble ridge. A man had narrowly escaped drowning there that very morning. There was much consternation, praise of Bob, and chiding of me among the party.

We dawdled home as I felt the most painful rheumatism. We paused to lean on every gate to admire the evening light on the hills and Chideock nestling between them. Helen, of course, was full of Bob's courage and envy at me being its cause.

Dicky is bringing Rex down on his motor-bike next weekend. I was thinking of Rex all the way home. It is just a year since we sat under the lamp in the drawing-room, reading Keats. I said I had a feeling we would not meet for ages and he said it couldn't be more than a year anyway, knowing he was to be articled to Father. I tell myself we have 'a very sensible relationship' as AVS put it.

August 24th.   Helen and I are reading *The Constant Nymph** aloud to each other, I think it is one of the cleverest and most delightful of novels imaginable. I've just finished *The Hand of Ethelberta* which I don't like as much as *The Trumpet Major.*†I had a nice present this week, from Denise, who sent me Francis Thomson's Poems, I did not know them; they have a sort of crystal beauty.

This afternoon a Mr Freeman came to see Father about Herman Melville. Father has just found the original of *Moby Dick* and wrote to the *Times Literary Supplement* about it; this has brought a flood of correspondence. Mr Freeman is writing a book about Melville for the *Great British Authors* series and so wants to discuss the discovery. He was a nervous man with a diffident manner. I felt he did not particularly want to talk to us girls so had no conversation with him.

* by Margaret Kennedy

† both by Thomas Hardy

After tea, Aunt Olive, Uncle Arthur, Helen and I set out to walk to
Golden Cap; we went to say goodbye to the rest, who were sitting on
the terrace. Father drew me aside to say "I think I should tell you that
Mr Freeman is the John Freeman who writes poems in *Georgian
Poetry.*"

For a moment, I could not think what they were, so smiled and said
something polite. Then I remembered; some of my favourite verses!
So I was able to be really interested when he asked me if I'd read
them. Someone remarked that though we are a literary family, we
have to call on our younger members when it comes to modern verse.
"Whereas the name Freeman is associated in my mind with history, it
reminds our young of poetry."

Mr Freeman replied "It's the youngsters who are right."

All laughed, and our party took its leave. How I wished I had been
able to tell him how I love 'Music Comes' and of course, he had left
by the time we returned.

August 25th. Today we went on a long talked-of expedition to
Symondsbury. A peculiar lane there is mentioned in a book we have
all been reading, *The Other End,** which makes us want to see it.

We all went except Mother, by a shady lane down, down to North
Chideock. The thatched cottages there were smothered in roses,
fuschias and holly-hocks, and the farm-yards filled with comfortable
ricks, blue waggons with red wheels, their shafts in the air, and cocks,
hens, geese and pigs.

Part of the way led by a stream flowing between beds of cresses,
willow herbs and tall grasses. After climbing a steep hill we came to
the lane in the book. It is certainly remarkable; narrow, between high
banks, almost cliffs, of yellow sandstone, on top of which hazels and
maples arched over the lane.

In the soft stone generations have cut their names or initials and
emblems such as hearts and crosses. There were texts: 'For us Jesus
died' and 'God is Love' in a crooked script and some weird little
pictures, one a neat carving of a bicycle. One large protuberance had
been cut into an ape's head.

There was an unearthly, supernatural effect in this lane, winding as
it were, underground, and lit by light far removed from the sun. We
came out by the conical hill with a hat of trees that we have long
wished to climb; one sees it from Bridport High Street. It was steep!
However, we eventually reached the top and lay and dozed in the
sunshine.

Miles of Dorset and blue sea stretched below and Symondsbury, a

* Short stories by Richard Earnshaw Roberts

34

pretty little village with a cruciform church, one or two big houses, a farm and cottages lay just beneath us.

We climbed down to the village and ordered lunch at the inn, which looked new, having been repaired within and without. Then we looked over the church, which is also under repair. The windows are being put in anew and two fine lepers' squints on either side of the nave unbricked. It is a fine old church.

The lunch was spread in a clean, airy room all to ourselves. The distant rumblings and mutterings of voices in the bar came most soothingly. Spotless linen, clean silver, a jug of delicious home-brew cider, a good salad and slices of corned beef garnished with parsley, new bread and a noble cheese made one of the best lunches I can remember.

So fortified, we returned home by the same route, Helen and I in front with Uncle Arthur, followed by my esteemed Aunt in a shiny alpaca jacket, antique skirt and a hat that defies description. Father looked an eminently respectable lawyer if ever there was one with his straw boater, black coat, grey trousers, and city boots. Aunt Olive, as usual, was elbowing him into the hedge as she talked. Uncle Arthur, in a heather-mixture sweater knitted by one of his many lady friends, bare-headed and tanned by the sun, does not match the others at all. It is hard to believe they are brothers and sister. I love him more and more each day.

We found that Father had forgotten to say we'd be out for lunch, so poor Mrs Cornish was still keeping it for us. Even this failed to annoy her. Really, she has the temper of a saint.

Mother actually said she felt she ought to pay some calls in return for the hospitality Helen and I have been receiving. I was deeply impressed at her giving up an afternoon's gardening for this detested ritual.

Helen was anxious to come as she had to return the hanky borrowed when her nose bled and hoped to see Bob Coombes. However, we called first at the Tolleys. Mrs Tolley was at home and took us round her lovely garden; it is sad to see the unfinished house; it would have been a large one.

We then went on to Plenty. A car in the drive and the hum of voices rather alarmed us but we were shown into the drawing-room. Miss Williams appeared and explained that there was a Women's Institute meeting in progress: would we join them for tea? We did so, among crowds of people but alas for Helen, no Bob! Afterwards we played bowls on the lawn; I thought it a fascinating game.

Then we went on to the Vicarage. The Lees were just setting off for a picnic supper. Mrs Lee and Mother sat in the garden while Helen, Edward and I played catch with a ball in the drive.

A telegram had come from Narney while we were out: 'Coming by 10.10 train tonight'. So Uncle Arthur hired a taxi and as a great treat I was allowed to go with him to Bridport to meet her. An orange moon hung over the sea; Uncle Arthur was most entertaining all the way.

The station was deserted, tomb-like in fact, and dark save for a few miserable gas lamps. At last the queerest train I've ever seen rattled in; one carriage and a long line of cattle-trucks. One lady and a small boy descended – no sign of Narney! We returned disconsolate; Mother was terribly disappointed. We assumed that Matron at the Radcliffe Hospital had cancelled her leave and all agreed that we should not like to be her patients that night!

August 26th.   Mother and I went by bus to see Helen off. I was sad to see her go, especially as Dicky and Rex can't come after all. Instead, Father has to go back to the office on Saturday. I suggested that I should go with him; I might see Rex in town, and the sooner I leave here the sooner I shall be able to get back to Somerset.

August 27th.   Narney arrived yesterday, unannounced. She has been trying to get to us since 5 a.m. on the 25th! She missed the connection at Didcot and had to return to Oxford. She has been telling me about operations, etc. at the Radcliffe; awfully interesting, though I felt a twinge of nausea at some of her descriptions.

We have made the most of her last day. She, Mother, Aunt Olive, and I took the 'bus to Charmouth and walked to Lyme along the cliff road. It really should be closed now; it has moved quite a number of feet in places and has great cracks in it. In one place it actually overhangs the sea.

Arrived at Lyme, we went on the Cobb. The sea was rough enough to break against it with clouds of spray and go washing back with a great swish and a gurgle. Yachts were putting out, one with red sails scudding before the breeze. A gaily-dressed crowd paraded up and down and people bathed in the blue waves below us.

The cliff road

In the afternoon we packed tea and took it to the beach at St Gabriel. Uncle Arthur lit a fire and boiled the kettle while the rest of us bathed. The sun had gone in and the sea was a dull grey, but we had a good bathe, jumping over the waves. Aunt Olive always bathes with her spectacles on and swimming breast-stroke looks exactly like a tortoise. Father, as usual, swam straight out to sea on his back and was no more seen until his return.

August 29th. Father and I left for London. It was sad to say goodbye, especially to my uncle. His farewell was a big kiss and "Goodbye Anne. I daresay you might be a shade worse."

CHAPTER IV

August 29th – September 25th, 1925

❧❦❧ ❦❧❦

*A*UGUST *29th.* At West Hill we found AVS, looking after my nephew Christopher for Rayne. It was lovely to see her again. As Captain Evans Smith says, I am a grass-spinster without her. 'Christer' is a jolly little boy, toddling unsteadily about, 'smiling all over' with large brown eyes, rosy cheeks and a mop of brown hair bleached fair on top.

I find it nice to be at West Hill again; the rooms look delightfully large and well-furnished after Hardown and, of course, the books and pictures are old friends. I remember some little thing about every part of the house – the stairs I tumbled down and the awful crash at the bottom; the corner in the dining-room where I was sent when I wouldn't eat my pudding and a thousand other places.

After tea, Father and I went to borrow some spoons and forks from our neighbours the Burrows, as the burglars have left us rather short and we have not yet collected the silver from the bank. Then we went a stroll, up West Hill and down Merton Lane.

I thought I was dreaming when I saw people walking in Mansfield Park [Kenwood Park] and the old ivy-fence gone. The park has been opened to the public and we went in ourselves. It was a beautiful evening and against the glow in the West tree-tops showed blue, the spire of Hampstead Parish Church pointing between them. Every moment the moon grew brighter and as we stood we heard the throb and roar of London, and the shouts and cries of people, softened by the still air.

August 30th. I took Christer a walk in Mansfield Park this morning and sat on a log to write. Christer talked softly to himself in his pram, and when I looked at him I saw him eagerly pointing and staring into a tree. I could see nothing there and suspect the young man sees many things that I miss; fairies perhaps.

In the afternoon, Father and I went to see the Bedingfields. It was a tremendous journey – we boarded a tram at the Camden Town

Britannia and went for miles and miles, out and out, through Holloway, Hornsey, Turnham Green and, at last, Palmers Green. We found the house eventually, though it was not easy among the streets of villas, new and exactly alike and the half-finished roads.

The Bedingfields have plenty of books and really fine pictures, some by Denise's mother and Bear's father and one good one by Bear himself. They also have an original Titian; it looked out of place in the small drawing-room, as it is a large nude. The lady reclines on a couch while her attendants search frantically in a chest for some clothing.

Father was made happy by the examination of a case full of old books; there was among other treasures an Elizabethan New Testament that was very quaint and delightful. While these were being looked at Bear fixed up his microscope and showed me a butterfly under it. The furrows on its wings were like a ploughed field. They kindly drove us home and had supper with us. I took them up to see Christer whom they deeply admired; he does look angelic when asleep.

September 1st.   Father and Dicky brought Rex back from the office this evening. It was lovely to see him and yet we were rather shy and embarrassed. However, after supper we played Bridge, Rex with his Aunt and Dicky with me. Then we played Slippery Ann, looked at books and arranged to go to Wembley together on Saturday, so the ice was well broken.

September 2nd.   This afternoon I dressed in my best and AVS took me to meet my dear Miss Attneave, who taught English at the Grove School. She awaited us in the Rest Room at Dickens and Jones, so AVS delivered me up and took her leave.

After a long discussion as to where to have tea we decided on Fullers. It *was* lovely to be with Miss Attneave again! She ordered a most sumptuous tea; Fullers do have good cakes; and we sat opposite one another and talked and talked and *talked*. She asked me about everyone in my letters, we discussed the Grove, I told her that I had given up the idea of being a Health Visitor and she said she was very glad, she told me about various mutual friends, and, oh, a thousand and one things. I felt gloriously happy, but she had a train to catch so we couldn't say half we wanted to. We walked down Regent Street, still talking, when my 'bus passed. We chased it and I leaped on with "Goodbye Anne, I'd like to take you home with me," from Miss Attneave, and "Well done, Miss," from the conductor. So it was over and I had plenty of time to remember the other things I had wanted to tell her.

AVS has had a letter from Mrs Dark saying that her niece has measles so she cannot have us back until the 26th. So goodbye to Joan Davy's visit! I am terribly disappointed as I have not seen Joan since she left the Royal School at Bath and she writes that she will be going to India with her parents next year. She and Helen are my best and dearest friends; I met them both at St Aldwyns School at Minehead when we were eight. I had been sent there as the Spanish 'flu was raging at West Hill and was miserably homesick. Joan was so kind and saved me from utter misery; I have loved her ever since. I did not see so much of Helen there but grew to know her when quite by chance, she came to the Grove School.

Rex's mother has invited AVS and me to visit them at Southampton before term begins, which will be delightful; only I shall not have any riding these holidays.

The Grove School

September 3rd. This afternoon I pushed Christer up to see Miss Lacey at the Grove School. A girl I remembered opened the door to No. 1 The Grove; I left Christer with her while I went upstairs to see if Miss Lacey was free.

With much fluttering at heart, I knocked at the well-remembered door, as I had done so many times before entering for the expected 'jaw'. The voice I knew so well said "Come in", and there she was in what seemed the same black coat and skirt, white shirt and black tie. Miss Fletcher, the assistant Head Mistress whom I always disliked, was, of course, with her.

They were anxious to see Christer and Miss Fletcher came down with me to fetch him. But he did not like her either. He burst into loud yells of protest. I think as well as Miss Fletcher the dark panelled hall frightened him. In the end I had to put him back in his pram and take him outside to the sunlight. Miss Lacey came down then and told several passing girls that "this is the son of an Old Girl". It was nice to see the dear old place again and the Grove with its lime trees. Nothing seemed changed, except perhaps myself.

September 5th. The day at the Wembley Exhibition. Rex came for me quite early, before I was ready, in fact, and we went by tube. It was a tremendous day. First, we went to Australia House, full of whirring machines and models of sheep farms, immense bins of corn and cases of fruit. Then to the Amusement Park, where, with great trepidation, we seated ourselves in the Giant Racer.

It was a terrifying experience! At first I was really frightened but it was a glorious fright and thoroughly enjoyable. After the first descent I was able to collect my senses and found that I was still alive. Rex confessed to keeping his eyes tightly shut the whole time.

Next, we went to His Majesty's Pavilion, which had fascinating models of ships of all ages, from the earliest canoe to our own *Dreadnought*. I especially liked a model of the *Revenge*.

This took us to lunch-time and we hurried back to see 'The Attack on Zeebrugge'. It was most stirring. A trumpet sounded and to a roll of drums the curtain parted to show Zeebrugge on a peaceful evening, the sun setting behind the town. The sea, reflecting the glow, lapped against the mole, where already a lighthouse twinkled. It grew dark, the moon rose and in its light we saw an iron-clad steal in like a ghost. It was just rounding the mole when there was a terrific explosion, and a huge flame shot up, revealing more ships coming in. The guns on the mole opened fire and we watched the battle. The *Invictor*, guarded by *Iris* and *Daffodil*, passed within thirty yards of the guns, shots pouring upon them. Clouds of sparks flew up and fell like golden rain. The noise was deafening and every now and then flares lit up a ghastly scene; the sea turned to blood and wrecks everywhere!

At last the curtain fell on the glare and destruction, lights went up, showing women in furs and wraps and men with bowlers and patent leather boots, and everything seemed flat, stale, mean, and uninspiring.

It was raining fast when we came out of the Pavilion; everywhere were shining umbrellas, greasy mud and fast-forming puddles in which the drops made little rings. We dodged the umbrellas as best we could and ran to the Palace of Art.

There were beautiful things to look at there; pictures, statues and pottery; but at last we tore ourselves away for tea in the Stadium. This was not pleasant owing to a large band of saxaphones blaring away all too near us.

Quite exhausted, we returned to Highgate. Before Rex left, we arranged to go to the National Gallery tomorrow.

September 6th. I met Dicky outside the bathroom door this morning and he asked if I would like a day in the country on his motor-cycle, to the Huts or to Rayne, perhaps? I thought it would be even nicer than the National Gallery, so after pumping up the tyres, etc. we went to fetch Rex from his rooms in Hornsey Lane. We decided on the Huts, though Rex wanted to go to Cambridge. I explained I had my oldest clothes on and was quite unfit to go there.

It was horrid crossing London, and when at last we were clear of streets it began to rain. However, we had a lovely lunch at Henfield – 2 fried eggs, tomatoes, and fried bread each and stacks of bread and butter.

It was delicious to leave the road and drive down the tiny lane to the Huts, bowered in greenery and with long lush grass on either side. Even though I have only been in London a week, it was good to be in the country again.

No one was at home at the Huts, which were built by the Black family out of railway carriages years ago and have been used by Blacks and Garnetts ever since. Uncle Arthur lives in the

The Huts

most attractive, thatched-roof one. It has an open brick fireplace, bunks for beds, and racks for guns.

It was more like June than September today, the grass knee-deep and wet with rain, and the trees overhead making one vast bower. We waded through the sappy growth to the pond. It was much over-grown and covered with brilliantly green duckweed. Even the Clayton's house was covered with briars – the whole place was like the garden of the Sleeping Beauty.

We munched sweet apples, picked up from the grass, and picked blackberries. Dicky went off with his gun to try for a rabbit while Rex and I visited the Guest House and the orchard.

Going home a different way we saw a remarkably fine sight as we approached the North Downs. A heavy black cloud overhung them and from beneath it the westering sun shot level rays, lighting every tree, bush and chalky outcrop with lurid colour. It was like a Constable painting. And what a glorious view from the top, when at last we had zig-zagged up between the steep chalk cuttings. All Sussex lay beneath us.

42

September 8th. I made an expedition to Keats' house this morning and felt I trod holy ground as I went down Keats walk. So it is, to me. I was on my way to an appointment with Cousin Jones, our dentist. He had plenty of Tatlers and an exceedingly beautiful young nurse. Also a cheerful flow of conversation that helped to allay the misery of his drill.

I read Conrad all the afternoon and was enraptured. He is the king of writers. And the afternoon post brought me a letter from Joan Davy, inviting me to stay at Farnborough and go on to Southampton from there. It is too lovely to be true! I posted my acceptance and then my brother-in-law, John, came in to see Christer and said that their German girl is ill with a septic throat and they cannot have him back for a while.

Kind, angelic AVS offered at once to stay on here with Christer which will mean her missing the Southampton visit. After John left, tears of disappointment came to her eyes. We can only hope that Lotta will get well quickly so that she can join me.

Rex came this evening, oddly early, I thought, and said when I opened the door "Well, what about the show?"

He had suggested our going to see a film *The She Devil* but I had thought no more of it. I was delighted and rushed off to get the necessary permission from parents and guardians.

They consented, and Rex and I gobbled our supper and set off. We went by tube to Leicester Square and found our way to the Capitol Cinema in the Haymarket. It was raining and London looked wildly beautiful with flashing whirring electric signs; reflections from cars and the brilliantly lit shops rippled in the oily road.

We had to watch a long series of films before at last, the She Devil appeared. She was a beautiful woman who had vowed she would see her husband's assassin dead at her feet. This aim was pursued with a truly awful intent, involving as it did the death of some hundreds of people.

We enjoyed it to the full and were much impressed by the film's savage beauty.

It is my last day in London, for tomorrow I go to the Davys. Mother took me to see *The Man with a Load of Mischief* at the Haymarket.

We lunched first at Eustace Miles' restaurant in the Tottenham Court Road; a dingy, ugly place, with dingy, ugly people gulping down their vegetarian dishes. Although the food was savoury and satisfying *when* it arrived, an hour later I was ravenous, as if I had had no lunch at all.

The play was very good – the bills called it 'A Romantic Comedy' and romantic it certainly was. It was a Georgian period-piece and the costumes were charming.

The Cast was; An Innkeeper ....Alfred Clark
                    His Wife....................Clare Greet
                    A Lady.......................Fay Compton
                    Her Maid....................Joyce Kennedy
                    A Nobleman................Frank Collier
                    His Man.....................Leon Quartermain

Mother could not hear well, so we bought the book of words. Coming home in the 'bus we discussed it thoroughly, Mother disapproving of the hero. But her own hero in her novel *The Infamous John Friend* is not an exemplary character.*

September 11th. Mother saw me off at Waterloo and after an uneventful journey I was met at Farnborough by Joan. Just the same, bless her, only with her hair in a becoming coil at the nape of her neck. She has grown up so naturally that it does not seem strange to find her living at home, her education finished. A less unaffected young lady would be hard to find; she is just my darling, merry, freckled Joan.

She had driven her car to the station herself but – to my secret relief – a youth from the garage drove us back.

Tudor House is delightful, with beautiful old furniture, delicate china and pretty chintzes and curtains. Mrs Davy, whom I hardly remembered, is as dainty and charming as her house. She is tall and slender with a lovely nose and eyes that crinkle at the corners like Joan's.

Major Davy and Tony are fishing in Ireland so I shall not see them. I would have liked to see Tony again, we used to go on birds' nesting expeditions together, he was a genius at finding nests. Mrs Davy soon went out to play tennis at the club, so Joan and I had tea together, with much to talk of after a separation of two years.

After dinner, we sat around the fire playing with George Robey, the spaniel. Alas, he found my hat – the one Mollie gave me – in the hall and practically demolished it. Joan and her mother thought it very funny; it was not their sort of hat; but though I joined in the mirth I could not help being rueful.

September 12th. I went with Joan on her driving lesson, sitting in the dicky with George Robey. Joan drove up a range of hills named Blackdown, where we had a good view over the heathey country around. Rhododendrons and firs are the trees with, of course, birches

* News of acceptance for publication of this book coincided with the diarist's birth. Her father, meeting the midwife on the stairs, was greeted with the good news. "Never mind that" he said, bounding past her; and throwing open the bedroom door, cried "Matty, your book has been accepted". The novel sold well, and was serialised on television in 1959.

and gorse. It is sandy, poor soil and the Army has spread its tentacles everywhere. There are soldiers at every turn, many roads are marked 'Private WD', and aeroplanes hum overhead all day long. But it is pleasantly open; we passed the hounds on a narrow bridge; nice to see a pack again!

Prince Henry is stationed here at present; Joan says he electrified Farnborough by coming to one of the sedate club dances as drunk as a lord and riding round the ballroom on a bicycle.*

We went blackberrying in the afternoon and again spent the evening round the fire. Mrs Davy told stories of her childhood, and of Joan and Tony when small. At breakfast Joan, aged six and her mouth full of porridge, asked "Have you ever committed adultery, Mummy?"

"No, darling, never."

Tony, his mouth also full: "Wouldn't it be awful if Mummy was to!"

September 13th.   I woke when the maid brought my tea to find pale sunlight streaming through the window, and outside robins were singing in a world of silver mist and sparkling dewdrops.

Mrs Davey went to church while Joan and I took George Robey a long, long, walk to the ground where the grand mustering of troops takes place. We crossed marshy places where there were willow herb, rushes, and fragrant mint. Then over a common full of wheel tracks and the marks of hooves. The mustering place is a huge grassy plain surrounded by pine woods; a white pavilion on one side is where Royalty sits to inspect its troops.

We talked chiefly of Army life, strange to me, all I know of it being gathered from Kipling. Joan told me of a proposal she had at a dance; it took her completely by surprise as she did not know the youth very well.

When she told her mother she was even more surprised to be told that "No girl need ever receive a proposal unless she wants it." She is still puzzled!

We had another walk in the evening with friends; the bells were ringing for Evensong and robins singing their piercing little dirges. There was a smell of wood smoke and decaying leaves and a tang of frost. Blue smoke from bonfires drifted lazily and golden light came in level rays between the trees; a peaceful walk.

Mrs Davy went out to dinner and Joan and I had a delightfully cosy evening. She played for me first, which I loved, for she plays very well. Almost the last time I saw her was at a concert at the Pump Rooms at Bath, given by girls from the Royal School; Joan and another girl

* Prince Henry, Duke of Gloucester, was the third son of King George V.

45

played Bach on two pianos. She was just as good tonight.

Afterwards we switched out all the lights but one corner lamp, made up the fire and sat one each side of the dancing flames. I went to bed feeling happy in our friendship.

September 15th. Mrs Davy, Joan, and George Robey all came with me in a taxi to the station and said goodbye in its musty depths. I had to change at Basingstoke, but it proved easy and at Southampton I immediately saw Mr Sangar, Rex's father, who had come to meet me. We proceeded to Shirley by tram, where his wife gave me a most affectionate welcome and after tea took me shopping.

They have a 'Shop Week' on, everyone has a numbered ticket left at the door and has to visit the shops to see if a free gift has been won. Then there are competitions in every shop, guessing the number of pages in a book, sweets in a jar, etc. Along the pavements 'Miles of Pennies' are growing; all this in aid of the hospital.

September 16th. A card came from AVS this morning to say that Christer has been returned to Rayne and John and that she will come today.

Mrs Sangar and I spent the morning in Bournemouth, going by train; we shop-gazed and lunched at Bobbys. It rained on the way but cleared to a fine breezy afternoon, so we walked to the pier. There were men fishing and steamers coming in to land their passengers. We stayed about an hour, it was so pleasant. At a bookshop on the way to the station they were selling off remainders and I bought a copy of Galsworthy's *White Monkey* for 3/6d.

We met AVS' train on our return; our taxi took a long time to reach Eskholme as we got stuck in the middle of the carnival. Long processions of decorated cars and lorries passed slowly, cowboys clattered up and down on horseback and people in fancy dress rattled tins up and down the dense crowds on the pavements.

September 17th. AVS and Miss Smythe, Mrs Sangar's sister, departed on a mysterious errand – to buy their presents for our hosts' silver wedding which is approaching. Miss Smythe is a very sedate little woman, always neat, her white hair smoothed into a bun and her shirt-blouse trimly inserted at the waist into her grey skirt. She is extremely 'proper' and Mr Sangar delights in teasing her at meals. "Oh Reggie, how can you!" she invariably replies, and his wife expostulates "Do leave poor Dora alone, Reggie."

He seems to know the whole of W.W. Jacobs by heart and we hear many of the Night Watchman's stories – not always very suitable ones! He is kindly giving me Bridge lessons, but I fear they are much above my head as yet.

I read the *White Monkey* this afternoon; good, but it could be better. I hope Galsworthy is not going to be content with the name he has made and slide into a groove; I fancied I saw signs of this.

September 18th. I have at last made up my mind to have my hair shingled, although I know that my parents and AVS dislike the fashion. But I have let it grow to please them and it is *still* only about three inches long! The trouble today was that I have no money and AVS precious little – not nearly enough for the jumper wool we were hoping to buy.

Last night AVS very sportingly offered to lend me enough to have my hair cut. I told her I had best go alone as she might interfere if she saw the hairdresser at work. She was much offended and we had a horrible row – ending in my going off to the hairdresser! This however was nothing to the scene on my return.

In the evening, shingled but very sore at heart, I went out alone. The sky was rich deep blue-black with powdery stars and down the street the lights threw green circles against the sky and yellow ripples on the wet road.

Suddenly everything stopped mattering – people, clothes, the fuss over my hair – everything went PHUT and there were just the sky, the stars, and the lights burning. I came back feeling as if I had been caught up in another world.

September 24th. At breakfast Mrs Sangar was making mystic allusions to something in the local paper and suddenly said "How would you like to take a trip to Southsea?" Naturally we were delighted and after lunch set out for the docks.

We boarded a steamer and were soon away. Southampton water was calm and blue though there were white clouds and a brisk wind. Soon the masts and rigging were left behind and we were passing wooded shores. It was interesting to see the different ships lying at anchor, and there were a great many sea-planes.

We passed the Isle of Wight and came to Southsea, a most unattractive town! AVS and I looked into shop windows and went to see the house where her grandparents used to live. She told me how her mother, then a beautiful young girl, fell in love with a young naval officer while living there. The match was forbidden and in pique she vowed she would marry the next man who asked her. This proved to the Rev. James Sangar, the new curate, a widower with five children in their teens.

She later had the mortification of knowing that her former sweetheart had risen to the rank of Admiral, while she reared seven children of her own on the slender stipend of her Rector husband.

We had tea at a café where there were wailing violins and a tinkling piano. Mrs Sangar and Miss Smythe had gone to see a friend.

But the trip back was glorious; to begin with the sky was like a sea of blood and all the ripples were crested with flames. Great clouds went rushing by as if they too, had caught fire as they passed the furnace of the sunset.

Then the colour died, the sky paled, darkened, and the land grew black where lights began to twinkle. The wind rose and passengers took refuge behind the funnel or went down to the saloon.

I went to the bows and stayed there, watching the lights ashore and on the ships and the winking buoys. One huge steamer passed very close, brilliantly lit, and we also passed the *Empress of France*. She was bound for America but had engine trouble off St Albans Head and was towed back for repairs.

The moon now shone on clouds like wool, the ripples caught her light and threw it one to another, and our steamer left a pale, bubbling track while our lights threw golden haloes on the sea.

I was bitterly cold but could not bear to leave and stayed there, watching the black land, the lights and the moon.

Miss Smythe came on a later boat as she left her scarf on the steamer we came in. Our return was made in the *Lorna Doone*, one Mrs Sangar and I had seen at Bournemouth. But poor Miss Smythe could not find her scarf.

September 25th. How kind Mr & Mrs Sangar have been during our visit! He had given so much time to my Bridge lessons, making up difficult hands for me to puzzle out, and his wife has been taking me about so much. She must have known how I longed for knitting-wool and had not the money, for today she took me into town and bought me 2lbs of the Bramble wool I was so attracted by at Bournemouth. Although she has said nothing, somehow I feel an extra warmth, as if she felt sorry for me over the ghastly hair-shingling row.

And Rex, to whom I sent some Chinese stamps by his mother, writes that I am to have the three-cornered Cape of Good Hope out of his duplicate book. I have spent most of today happily knitting – our last day here.

CHAPTER V

September 26th – December 23rd, 1925

❧❊❦❧ ❦❊❦❦

SEPTEMBER 26th. Today, home again. It *was* a journey; we had to change at Westbury, Castle Cary, Durston, and Taunton. Our train from the last was packed, it being market-day, and we had to travel apart. I had two farmers next to me and enjoyed their discussion on crops and the weather, and observations on every field that we passed.

Brewers Water awaited us with spotless rooms; tea set out on a snowy cloth, and an amiable Mrs Dark, thank heaven! AVS dropped rather a brick by complimenting her on her health. She replied plaintively that she was "Not too bad", and explained her rosy cheeks by being "flushed with the wind".

The farm-yard smelt as only a Somerset farm can; clean, sweet and delicious. I am sleeping above the sitting-room and so have miles and miles of heavenly Somerset country spread below me. To my surprise and annoyance the window has been covered with wire-netting. My bed is directly under it, and as I always sleep with it open, AVS had given instructions by post. She has always been nervous of my sleep-walking habits, but I don't think I ever do it now.*

September 27th. After church at Stogumber this morning Archer told us that there are five boys at Hartrow this term, of whom he and David are the only ones we know, Guy having gone up to Oxford. Hartrow won't be Hartrow without Guy, he has been there so long. We walked to Nurse's with Miss Hall and met Mollie by the way. She is having a holiday between jobs and seems undecided about her next one, but is as blooming and full of beans as ever – and of Mrs Webb!

She came to tea, and she and I walked to Bicknoller afterwards. I

---

* On one occasion, after a walk of about 14 miles, the 8 year-old Anne was discovered trudging round her bedroom, muttering in her sleep "I can't go any further!" At the Grove school she was once rescued while asleep in the act of climbing out of a high window.

was excited at seeing the Evans Smiths again; thank heaven they were in. Mrs Evans Smith told me to call the Captain for tea; he was in the top field cutting thistles. With him were four hound puppies they are walking. Such darlings; Gardner, Genius, Garter and Grock. Garter is the bitch, the largest, and Grock a clownish little mite, weak and puny.

I was taken round the stable and introduced to three new ponies. They still have Mildmay, Prudence, Watershed, Filbert, Heatherbloom, and The Dun.

We had a very jovial tea (our second); there were so many things to talk about. I am glad to say they like my newly-shingled hair very much. After the terrible scene with AVS [when I had it cut without telling her], this was comforting.

It was a perfect evening, the sunshine gilding tree-tops and roofs; the Quantocks in their russet autumn coats. The bells were ringing for Evensong, and on the stable-doors robins trilled softly. The puppies tumbled about in the yard, and the ponies went "crunch, crunch-crunch" steadily on with their feed of sweet hay.

Every step home was a joy, I was so happy. The light looked almost *thick*, it was so golden; there was a sort of glamour over everything, the level sun-rays making a mist.

Gordon fetches the cows

September 28th. I went to Elworthy today, arriving about 11.0. Poor little Gordon has fallen off a cart and dislocated his elbow. He has to have painful treatment that makes him scream; I listened to an account of his sufferings, and a long tirade against Dr Webb. I wonder why it is always the doctor's fault when things go wrong?

Edith Stephens was at the cottage when I called there, on her holiday. She has grown into such a pretty girl. The doll I gave her when we were five is still in its glass case on the dresser; she has never been allowed to play with it. I hope she will be my maid one day as we've always planned; if I ever marry, that is.

Back at Whites Farm I had dinner, sitting in the settle and partaking of home-cured bacon, pickled cabbage, and bread and butter. I went to the Middletons for tea. All the cats have died save Miss Brown, and Savage has a fat sprawling puppy. The foxhound puppy Singwell died, but Spaniard has grown into a splendid hound.

Mrs Hayes and Gordon walked to the top of Ashpier with me and after that I wasn't long reaching home.

September 29th. The first day of term. Miss Ford put her head from the train as I looked for a carriage; she said "Mr Browne has forsaken us; we haven't seen him for months." I swallowed hard and said I expected he was still on holiday. But it is late for holidays – suppose he should be ill? Miss Webster had arrived at school, as beautiful as ever. There are four new girls.

October 3rd. I rode Heatherbloom today, and fell off when she shied, as I was riding without stirrups. I was not hurt, and jumped up to catch her, brushed off the mud and rode on. Soon my elbow began to smart, and I found I had grazed it rather badly.

The Evans Smiths were out when I got back, and not knowing if they expected me to lunch, I decided I had best go home. No sooner had I got through the village than I met them, and it was evident that they had expected me to stay. When I reached Brewers Water I found that AVS had finished her lunch and was rushing off to meet Mollie and go with her to Elworthy. A car had been ordered so she could not wait for me.

I got myself some food in a listless sort of way and ate it dejectedly. My head ached, my elbow was smarting, and the house still as a grave. Lying on my bed I felt miserable; though usually I like being alone I felt wild at the thought that at that moment I might have been laughing at Bicknoller.

I soon fell asleep – and there was a knock at the door and in rushed Mollie.

They could not have the car till 5.30, she said, and as AVS seemed to be fretting about me, she had come to fetch me. Really, we two should be tied together with apron strings, she has never known such a pair! So I was soon bustling about getting ready, and we set off for Stogumber.

It was the anniversary of their brother's death in the war and the car had been ordered to take flowers for his memorial tablet in Elworthy church. I remember the day well; AVS giving me lessons in the Rectory schoolroom, and her mother coming in with stricken face and the telegram in her hand.

The mist had cleared now, and everything was bathed in a rosy light, the sky a soft blue with fleecy pink clouds. We found the Hayes still at tea and joined them at the table.

It was a horrid meal as Mrs Hayes insisted, in a high pitched voice, in enlarging on the sufferings imposed upon Gordon, to her mind largely through Dr Webb. AVS stiffened and grew 'glarey'. [i.e. with glassy eyes and pursed mouth, all too well known to me.] Mrs Hayes persisted; Mollie and I tried to laugh it off, and Ned to soothe, but to no avail. It was unpleasant.

I was thankful when we left to arrange the flowers in the church. Though there is nothing remarkable about tiny St Martins I am fond of it. AVS's father used to preach in a black gown on hell fire and eternal damnation to great effect; I needed a great deal of soothing reassurance before I could go to sleep after Evensong and one of those sermons! There is a seventeenth century inscription with Tudor roses painted over the chancel arch: 'O Lorde Prepare Our Arts to Praye'.

Our return to the farm was happier; Ned and Gordon were just setting out to see the sheep, so I joined them. It was already dusk and the orchard dark as we went through. On the hill it was lighter and I was able to admire a marvellous crop of mangolds, and fine fat lambs – or hogs I should say. From the sunset our shadows lay long and black across the dewy grass and the pink light still touched hedge-tops and our faces.

It was dark when we got back but Ned wanted to show me his hay. I had to guess its quality by the smell! Then we shut up the fowls and I ran to fetch the lantern. By its light I was shown the wood pile; stack upon stack of beech and ash logs, and piles of faggots. An old joke of Isaac's is that the ashen faggot, burned on Xmas Eve till its withy-band is consumed and before the cider is allowed to be drunk, was by a wag bound with an iron chain, so that the company waited well past midnight for their drink.

It was milking-time and I wanted to milk Buttercup again, but just as we were fetching the pails the Maxwell's horn sounded. Mollie and AVS were sitting amicably by the back'us fire with Isaac on the settle, Mollie on the 'coopy stool'.* The wide hearth, black sooty kettle in the huge chimney, bacon hanging round, and the open oven-door were all lit by the leaping flames, the rest of the cluttered room in cavernous shadow.

October 4th. It was Harvest Festival at Stogumber. AVS and I went to church at 8.0, and again for Evensong. It was *packed.* We were wedged in at the back, very hot from the press and at least a hundred candles steadily burning in the huge brass chandelier. There was a strong smell of apples and Sunday clothes. Everyone sang lustily and Mr Couch preached lustily too, waving his arms in Celtic excitement; he gets very Welsh at times. We sang the Te Deum at the end of the

* A small milking stool

service; the rich old words seemed to match the colours of flowers and fruit, the hot smell, and the candlelight. It should always be sung like that.

October 10th. Still no sign of Mr Browne. I miss the interest of looking out for him badly. Another architect comes in his place, and Chris, the Williton station-master's son, asked him "How's the Taunton chap?" "Oh, he's still bad", returned the other. Apparently he has been ill for a month. And how can I return the book he lent me?

Miss Ford says that Chris has developed an interest in me. This morning he got into my carriage and began to talk, which, as I was trying to do my prep., was a little trying. However, he was amusing; I asked how he enjoyed *Sense and Sensibility* which he has to read for his English examination. "Oh, its all right for *girls* I suppose, but I don't think much to it."

October 17th. I found Mrs Evans Smith and her sister gardening this morning; the Captain was out on his new motorbike but would ride with me on his return. I cut the grass and did some odd jobs: he didn't come and didn't come. His wife grew quite worried; he hasn't had the bike long, could he have had an accident?

At last he arrived; had never said he would be riding, had only been where he said he was going, no, he had not had an accident. His temper was not improved by Heatherbloom rolling in her bedding just as Paul had finished dressing her. "You filthy little beast – damn your eyes – I'll teach you – you little swine" etc. I love him when he is angry! Of course I tactfully withdrew, and when at last be brought the mare out, saddled, bridled, and shining like satin, he had quite recovered and actually walked up the drive to open the gate for me.

David brought Peter, the Hartrow grey, down to be clipped in the afternoon and he and I took turns to turn the handle while Captain Evans Smith did the clipping. David has grown, and was a marvellous sight in wondrous breeches, fancy stockings with red tassels, a brilliant pull-over, and long scented curls waving in the breeze. When taxed with having a cold later, the Captain remarked that at any rate he could smell young Holden's hair!

Halfway through our operations Mr Sweet Escott arrived on his new mare, another grey; naturally he had a long gossip which delayed matters. The Captain told Mr Sweet Escott to put three guineas onto David's bill for instruction in horse-clipping, and Mr Sweet Escott entreated him to run the clippers over David's hair.

After a hilarious tea I was given a ride on the new Dartmoor pony. He is only just broken and full of mischief, but was quite good till he suddenly bucked me off in the middle of the village. Luckily it was on the grass by the school so I was not hurt.

October 21st. Mrs Dark has given AVS notice again. She has done this so often that AVS has told her it will only be taken if in writing from Mr Dark. Mr Dark is highly amused.

The West Somerset Foxhound's Opening Meet at St Audries is now a matter of burning concern; I think Mr Sweet Escott will probably offer to take me, as he said he will be hunting. But AVS does not want me to follow on foot all day alone, and, even worse, it would mean missing a day at school. This is much disapproved of, especially by Miss Webster, as I am working for school certificate. Kind Mrs Evans Smith and her sister tried their best to persuade AVS on my behalf today, pointing out that the young should be allowed all the pleasures possible, as they are bound to meet disappointments and crosses later – a point of view I heartily endorse! Then the Captain said: "Shall I go in and plead for you?" He came out, saying in a sepulchral voice "It's working, it's working!"

In fact, it worked so well that AVS said she'd see, and I knew that spelt consent.

Walking home – AVS comes to Bicknoller with me now as she disapproves of my being out alone after dark – we discussed the matter. Then the happy idea of inviting Keren Wood to come with me to the meet occurred to AVS. This should solve all problems.

October 22nd. I am terribly disappointed. Mrs Wood won't allow Keren to miss school. And there is no word from Mr Sweet Escott. So that is that. . .

November 7th. AVS and I went to a meet at Curden today; that is, AVS went so far and was then deterred by a muddy field of cows. She had already been doubtful of my shortcuts across country, and to tell the truth I was rather relieved when she turned back.

I followed a horseman through Curden Wood, large and dark with a pungent smell of decay, and came out in a meadow. And there was Curden Farm with its ricks and barns, and just beyond, a mass of pink and black coats, brown, bay, grey, and chestnut horses, and the waving sterns of the foxhounds.

I recognised the Kershaw girls, David on the new mare, Corney on Queenie, and Mr Blowfeld from Dunster, among others.

They drew Curden Wood and we foot-folk climbed to the top of the hill. We could see the various villages, Samford Brett, Bicknoller, and Stogumber, each with its church tower and thatched roofs, and all the green meadows and red ploughed fields, the elms bare now save for a few golden leaves. The Quantocks too, all copper-coloured, and away in the distance the muddy brown Channel and the blue ridges of Exmoor. Over it all great storm-clouds were rolling up, blotting everything with their loads of rain.

Presently hounds began crashing about in the wood, and then came a whimper, followed by the ringing peal of the whole pack in full cry. Mr Dalzell, who had come into the field on Filbert, had a job to calm him down; he pricked his ears and reared at the tingling sound.

Suddenly a fox popped out at the corner of the field, saw us, and popped back again. Seconds later there was a flood of hounds, tumbling over one another in a mass of pied and tan and waving sterns. Then a long scream: "Gone Away-ay-ay" from the other side of the wood. Away flew all the riders, cramming down their hats. They jumped a hedge into the next field and were flying over that when a man yelled "Young grass! Come back!" The girl leading, I think Peggy Kershaw, reluctantly reined up and they all went round by the hedge.

There was a check at the next spinney and those left behind were able to catch up. Hounds whimpered in the undergrowth and Charlie Back was urging in the slackers, the crack of his whip like gun-shots. Then we saw Reynard steal out and race across some plough, a tiny red speck. A man whooping "Tally Ho!" saw him double back and rode him with uplifted crop, but the fox dodged him and re-gained the spinney.

Evidently they lost that fox, as there was a long pause and then the clop, clop of riders on the road below. They went to Vellow and we soon saw some on the skyline a mile away. An old man in shiny leggings and an enormous umbrella lent me his field-glasses and I watched for a while. But nothing more happened so I came home.

The Elworthy postman, Pattimore, brought us a note from Mrs Hayes in the afternoon. Dear old Isaac has had a slight stroke. He was in Square Mead and fell down; unable to rise he shouted for Ned, who luckily, was in the next field hauling mangolds, and who brought him home in the cart.

Poor dear old man! I've loved him for so many years, ever since I was little, and used to have such good times with him digging potatoes, making a bonfire of the weeds and roasting the largest spuds.

November 14th. Today was Isaac's funeral. We went with Sully from the garage and his mother, Sully being the undertaker. Elworthy Church was crowded; the service very impressive. The bearers were all local men whom Isaac had known well.

But the most beautiful part was by the grave. Everyone wept, and each word Mr MacTaggart said went floating into a frozen stillness. Not a leaf stirred; it was as if the trees and hills were listening. It seemed right and natural as they let the coffin down between Isaac's wife and the two sons already lying there, among the fields he knew so well.

It was the first funeral I have been to; I felt that death is not terrible, but peaceful and natural.

Mrs Hayes signed to us to go to Whites Farm, so after speaking to Mrs Middleton we did so. There were three tables in the dining room, each groaning under the weight of food. One was for the men, and had a huge joint of beef, pickles, and foaming jugs of beer, while the others were laid with cakes, bread and butter, jams, cream, junkets, and stewed fruit.

There was a roaring fire and everyone began to cheer up. Poor Gordon, who cried as if his heart were broken in church, was quite comforted by all the food and warmth. We too were glad to get near the fire and thaw our frozen feet.

It was a real, old fashioned funeral-feast. Ned and Mrs Hayes bustled about, talking to each in turn; Mrs Welsh, Mrs Besley, and Mrs Rutt dispensed the tea. I enjoyed seeing Ned's nieces, Dolly and Louey again; they used to be my playmates when they lived at Lower Tilsey.* They had the cottage of Tom Faggus†, the highwayman, with his initials cut in the oak cupboard door. Louey has grown tall and graceful, with the attraction country girls always seem to have. She has piles of glorious hair coiled up on her head. Dolly has lovely hair too, but in a plait as yet.

We were introduced to Harry Hayes, of whom we've often heard but never met. We all got to reminiscing about Isaac and how he used to spoil me, letting me feed the fowls at all hours, and giving me surreptitious sips of cider.

Mrs Hayes of course told us the details of the illness; Isaac was cheerful and talkative till he became unconscious two days before he died. Another nice thing is that everyone he was fond of happened to visit him within a few months of his death. We were there two days before, Harry and his family were staying at the farm six weeks ago,

* Issaac moved his family there when he gave up his job as game-keeper. He and his wife reared their seven children in the tiny gamekeeper's lodge at Higher Tilsey. It was buried in woods, reached only by a track, and measured about 10 x 12 feet. The older children slept in tents in the summer, and rode to school at Brompton Ralph on donkeys. Though so fearfully cramped, Isaac told Anne that his wife was heart-broken at leaving and always yearned for her microscopic home.

† He features in fictionalised form in *Lorna Doone*, by R.D. Blackmore.

and other relatives came then, including his older brother Joseph, whom he had not seen for years. We found this very comforting.

When we left, dear Ned, his eyes moist, kissed me, saying "Oh, Miss Anne, don't mind me."

AVS said she could not help thinking, as we waited in church for the funeral party, of Isaac's probable remark, were he able to make it: "Drat the boy, he be late vor my funeral!"

November 16th. When I left the train Mrs Hayes was on Stogumber station, seeing Harry off to Bristol. Poor dear, she was upset at his going and at the thought of home with only two faces instead of three. She came up and lunched with us, and we showed her photographs of people she knew till she cheered up, and then we walked to Stogumber with her.

November 17th. Mother came today; she is staying till Saturday when Keren comes for the weekend. She arrived while I was at Bicknoller. Mrs Evans Smith was half asleep before the fire, but roused herself to tell me exciting news. They have a pupil, a boy named Dudley Frost, who has just returned from the Argentine. Then sad news; poor little Gardner caught cold and died last night, though Mrs Evans Smith sat up with him till 3 o'clock.

Presently the Captain and the pupil came; Mr Frost is quite a presentable young man. We did not speak much till we were all riding down the lane; Captain Evans Smith on a new brown pony, Mr Frost on Conga the little chestnut, and I on Punch.

We had some good galloping on Woolston Moor while the brown pony was schooled – a sudden thrill being occasioned by Conga who took it into his head to lie down and roll. Mr Frost only just got off in time. Before we left I was told to take Punch down to the bottom of the Moor and see if I could get a gallop out of him. He simply flew. It was a heavenly gallop.

It was a heavenly evening, too. The sun was just dipping behind the hills and the Quantocks looked a rich claret, with velvet-purple shadows. As we rode home a silver slip of crescent moon shone above the glow. Mr Frost hastily turned over the money in his pocket.

He very reluctantly allowed me to un-saddle Punch, but refused to let me carry the tack to the harness room, saying it was too heavy. I hope he won't continue like that. AVS was sipping tea with Mrs Evans Smith by the light of candles in tall silver sticks and a blazing fire, James Pigg and Pye curled up at their feet.

We were lit by the wisp of the moon all the way home, the glow in the west fading as the moon brightened. And when we got in, there was Mother, reading by the fire.

57

November 19th. After a hasty lunch we all three repaired to our rooms to beautify ourselves. There was a meeting at Halsway Manor to decide on a course of lectures. These are to be given on literature, by a Canon Yates.

We arrived to find Mr Mitchell knocking out the shag from his pipe on the stone gargoyles of his princely porch, and welcoming the various carloads of arrivals. As we had walked, we felt humble, but Mother really looked very posh in her fur-lined coat, so we took courage and marched in with the best.

The meeting – about fifty of us – was held in a large panelled hall; a beautifully carved overmantel had a design of lions rampant. Mrs Evans Smith came and sat with us in front, so that Mother could hear.

Canon Yates briefly sketched out the different courses he could give us; we voted, and I'm glad to say that Poetry had it. The rest of the meeting was taken by Mr Mitchell, who counted the votes as to where the lectures would be held, at what time, etc. It was decided to have them at Williton at 3.30 on Wednesdays.

The Canon then concluded by an apology for taking time up with lectures that would otherwise be occupied in hunting!

November 21st. Keren arrived by the 9.45 train, already dressed for riding, so we started for Bicknoller at once, AVS and Mother coming too. Going along Kensie Lane Keren and I rehearsed the quarrel scene from *Julius Caesar,* which we are to act at the school concert. Our audience seemed to find it amusing.

We rode with Dudley Frost, he on Filbert, Keren on Punch, and I on Conga. We had good gallops on Woolston Moor where we jumped over and over the stream. Conga was very full of beans, and nearly had me off once or twice by suddenly bucking in mid-gallop, most disconcerting. Then we hacked along to Vellow and Stogumber. Mr Frost was amusing on the way home, anxious to show us what a man of the world he is, the various revues he has been to, and how he has been "behind the scenes".

November 22nd. Keren and I took the farm dogs on my favourite walk this afternoon – the woods by Heddon Oak. They are especially lovely now, with a few orange or russet leaves on the boughs and a delicious carpet of crisp, rustling leaves underfoot.

It is really winter, the holly berries red, only a few hips and haws left by the birds, and the bracken that has stood so long lying in russet heaps.

As we were coming home the dogs rushed into a bush, barking furiously. To our consternation a large cock pheasant flew out. Puppy and Susan tore after it, though we yelled with all our might. They soon caught it, and Puppy, wagging her tail and beaming with pride, brought it and laid it at our feet. It was quite dead.

Had the dogs caught and killed the Infanta of Spain our consternation could not have been greater. We stood and stared: the pheasant seemed to stare back, as if to say "You've done it now!" Then we began to laugh, and laughed and laughed till we literally ached. It was the dogs' turn to stare then! We were terrified at being seen with the corpse but could not think how to dispose of it. We thought of throwing it into the pond but it was too shallow. At last we covered it with leaves at the foot of a tree. When we passed anyone on our way I blushed and Keren giggled, so guilty did we feel.

Mr Dark took it very calmly and laughed at our fears. There had been a shooting party yesterday, and he had no doubt that this was a wounded bird that had crept into the bush to die. Mrs Dark and AVS went undercover of night to retrieve it, but failed in their search. So we lost an excellent dinner through our foolish fears.

December 5th. Filbert, who was thoroughly nappy, put me down on Woolston Moor while Mr Frost and I were galloping today. I don't know what he did, but I suddenly found myself falling, falling, while a huge green earth rose to hit me with a BANG. I got up instantly, and there was Filbert executing a sort of dance with his hind legs over his head, and galloping madly towards the road.

A boy driving cows ran to stop him and Mr Frost galloped in pursuit, but he reached the road just as a car came round the corner. It looked as if nothing could avert a collision, but he swerved, and galloped on. I picked up a stirrup leather lying on the ground and ran. Mr Frost returned, much concerned as to my welfare, but my rage with Filbert convinced him that I was not hurt.

He waved a car down, and two dear old ladies gave me a lift. Horrible visions of a mangled horse and damaged car ahead floated in my mind. Thanking the ladies, I got them to stop at the Bicknoller lane, and pounded up it gasping fears and prayers. I turned a corner – and there was a carter leading Filbert towards me. He was unscathed and much more sedate as I put on the leather and mounted.

December 13th. I can't understand people not liking the country in winter. There are so many colours – dark red of ploughed fields, so marked against yellow-grey stubble, russet of the bracken, purple-crimson of bare twigs, brilliant emerald of ferns and mosses, and iron-grey and indigo of the skies. The stormy dawns and sunsets just now seem to mingle; they come so close that their colours never seem to fade completely. And I love the long nights too, the blue-black sky with teeming stars, the wind 'soughing'; frost in the air, and then the moon.

December 21st. My seventeenth birthday. I hurried downstairs and found quite a collection of letters and parcels. Father has sent me Masefield's *Collected Poems.* Helen, a little wallet full of stamps and a letter. She says she has sent Christmas cards to the Tolleys and to Bob Coombes.

December 23rd. It snowed heavily all yesterday, which kept me indoors. Today a clear blue sky and sunshine sparkling on the clean white world.

We are removing to Nevis, another farm, for Christmas, as Mother and Father are coming, and Dicky – who will be staying at Elworthy – and it is too much for Mrs Dark.

I went down with some of our luggage, the lamp-globe for one thing, and had a difficult walk as the roads were sheeted with ice; it took me a long time to reach Nevis, a thatched farm-house in the Kingswood lane.

We went there for tea, taking a few necessaries as the roads are impossible for the horse and cart to fetch our luggage. We wondered if Dicky could possibly get here in his Baby Austin.

About six o'clock we heard a car, and rushing to the window beheld a diminutive vehicle, more like a perambulator than a car. Then came a knock at the door, and Dicky's voice: "Is this Mrs Maddock's?" The travellers were quite warm and comfortable, but glad to arrive. They had set out from London at 10 a.m. and only stopped once, at Salisbury for lunch.

It is cosy and comfortable here, the sitting-room larger than at Brewers Water. We miss the light and the view, as the windows here are old casement ones with leaded panes and the room is rather dark. Mother, AVS and I have to share a bedroom, AVS and I in one bed, a large one fortunately.

Dicky left for Whites Farm after supper; he is to stay a week. AVS is writing to Mr Sweet Escott to suggest his exercising Peter, as all the boys are away.

CHAPTER VI

Christmas Day, 1925 – February 22nd, 1926

❧❧❀❀ ❀❀❧❀

*C*HRISTMAS DAY. *At Nevis Farm (Mrs Maddock's) Kingswood.*
I got up early to go to Church. Through the night I was conscious
of distant bells ringing joyfully, giving a hazy Christmas feeling to my
dreams. This was enhanced by the weird effect of dressing by
candlelight and groping my way out into a wintry world. It had been
raining and the road was slushy over the ice, but the fields still showed
white as the dawn slowly broke. The warm church, lit by scores of
candles, made a strong contrast. I walked home quickly to a delicious
breakfast of sausages.

Dicky arrived in time for a regular Christmas dinner of roast goose,
plum pudding, and mince pies. Afterwards we had 'the hamper', a
suitcase this year, and I dispensed the presents. I had a new stamp
album, some very nice books, and something from all my friends.

The parents seemed disposed to sleep, so AVS and I went up to
Elworthy with Dicky after tea.

We found that Mrs Hayes and Gordon had gone to church, but
Ned was in the yard 'feeding up', very behind with all the work owing
to the deep snow. There was a much heavier fall up here and it was
still lying.

The kitchen at Whites Farm

We had a very jolly evening. Ned came in to a delicious tea and Dicky played with Gordon, much to his delight. He had brought him some balloons, a new bladder for his football, and a dreadful thing that blows up to about five feet to hit some unsuspecting innocent in the face.

Dicky drove us home and took Gordon too. The snow, deep at the top of Ashpier, had disappeared when we had dropped eighty feet, and the fog too, leaving a clear sky.

December 27th. Father and I went on a long long walk today. We went up Crowcombe; one can see the tall silver trunks of the beeches and network of boughs and twigs against the red-brown hills. We walked along the top of the hills and came down at Halsway. Father told the most remarkable stories the whole way and kept me in roars of laughter, so that I staggered along with aching sides. We arrived home half an hour late for dinner, but no matter.

December 28th. Mr Sweet Escott offered Dicky a day's hunting on Peter today, which I am glad of. And at Bicknoller I found a whole cavalcade ready to start; the Captain, Paul, Winter, and Mr Frost on the well-bred but hot little chesnut, Girlie.

I rode Conga, having saddled him myself, and was told to tighten his girths before ascending Quantock Moor. Conga jumped up and down like an electric eel and would not let me re-mount. I was left behind with Paul by the time I got one foot in the stirrup, and was hopping round hanging on to his mane. At last I swung myself up, but before I could get my other leg over Conga bucked and there I was huddled on his neck in the most absurd way.

I hung on by the skin of my teeth and at last managed to get seated, upon which Conga rushed up the hill at full gallop. However, it is very steep there so he was soon blown, and quite subdued by the time we joined the others on the long high flat above Staple Plain. I rode Sunstar and led Conga quietly about with Paul also leading and the dogs and hound pups at our heels, while the others galloped in the heather. We saw them looming through the fog like ghostly highwaymen.

I rode home leading Conga and feeling very proud. Mr Frost ran me back to Nevis in his car; I spent a fidgety time after tea expecting Dicky, who had promised to take us to the famous pantomime, *Robinson Crusoe,* at Watchet. The Evans Smiths and many of our friends were in it and have been rehearsing for weeks. Suppose Dicky had ended his hunt miles away, and was still wearily hacking back to Hartrow!

Suppertime came; we changed our clothes and still no Dicky. AVS and I decided to walk to Stogumber and order a car; we should perhaps meet the Baby Austin on the way. Mother resigned herself to staying at home and we set out. A little way along the lane a car came up – Dicky. I rushed back for Mother, we all bundled in, and reached the hall at Watchet in ample time, getting excellent seats.

Dicky was wearing an entire suit borrowed from Ned, as he was soaked by the time he got back, and was, also, very stiff after being in the saddle from 9.0 a.m. till 5.30. He had had a good day – the staghounds met at Quantock Farm and they moved fast all day, no hanging about in the rain as I had feared. Major Mott, who combined being actor-manager, composer, and author of the pantomime with the part of Mrs Crusoe, was a perfect Dame. The scenario was all local, a hunt in progress during the first scene. The next was the interior of the village 'bus, the third the bar at the Carew Arms, Crowcombe. Act II was a desert island – Flatholm, – with Robinson (the Captain) disguised in furs and a parasol. The entire cast was then taken to the bottom of the sea in a lift, and entertained by seductive mermaids.

The Bad Fairy (one of the Motts) having broken the lift, the Good one landed them at Doniford, from whence 'Ida the Glider' took them in her 'plane to the last act at the Carew Arms once more.

Mrs Evans Smith, as Lady Heathfield, wife of a millionaire, was superb in pink satin, a tulle scarf, immense pearls, and a lorgnette. Her songs were splendid and apart from some old favourites, composed by Major Mott.

The next pantomime is to be *Cinderella* at Stogumber; the Kershaws are much involved in it and Mrs Evans Smith again has the lead. St John Couch, the Bicknoller vicar's son, is to be Prince Charming, and his uncle, our vicar Ambrose Couch, the stepmother.

I hear it is to be quite an elaborate show with hired costumes and a large chorus. Peggy Kershaw has asked me to do programmes for it.

December 29th. I found Mrs Evans Smith frantically assembling her clothes for the dress rehearsal tonight and sucking a raw egg for her throat. I washed up the accumulated dishes from three meals and then helped make the Captain's costume, sewing on hooks and eyes and elastic, and making black velvet paws for his Felix costume. He said "By gum, I wish you were my daughter!"

December 30th. Mr Frost and I talked most amicably today as we rode round Monksilver and Stogumber. I felt like Zoggs when she met the disguised Robinson in the pantomime: "I shall never forget dear, dear Rob (sniff sniff) but I may as well console myself with this very nice young man".

63

We arrived at Stogumber school-room before the doors opened and were admitted through the Green Room where we caught sight of a heated Captain making up a row of girls.

It soon appeared that there were not nearly enough seats. Men and boys who were shut out began to grumble and mutter in a dense crowd outside the door. Halfway through the performance they got it open enough to throw in a handful of mud but were finally quelled by Hutchings, our august red-haired butcher. He went out in the most courageous manner and after that things were quieter.

'Amby' Couch made a gloriously conceited step-mother; two of the GFS girls were the ugly sisters and displayed their catty natures admirably. St John was every inch a Court exquisite and Mrs Evans Smith looked and sounded youthful and charming. A very good show. I found the twenty-three programmes I did were the only ones available.

December 31st. A very disconsolate Cinderella lay in bed today, with a splitting headache and a strong feeling that last night's performance was a dismal failure; she thought the muttering at the back of the hall had been meant for her. I speedily reassured her, got cold bandages and various remedies and she began to cheer up.

It was actually fine for my ride – a little sunshine amid all the rain. I stayed for lunch, which I dished and washed up; tended the invalid, made up the fire and set an iron upon it to press the clothes for *Robinson Crusoe* tonight. Mrs Evans Smith seemed so poorly that the Captain suggested I had better learn her part. However, instead Mr Frost and I rode to Stogumber to try and retrieve Lady Heathfield's pearls, somehow lost during *Cinderella*. We tried the school, Mr Févre the schoolmaster, and the Kershaws, in vain. We disgraced ourselves at the last-named as Conga and Girlie ate large quantities of creeper off the porch and Girlie left hoof-marks on the lawn.

January 1st, 1926. A pouring wet New Year; too wet for a projected gallop on Elworthy Burrows, we exercised in the riding school. I have never seen such rain; it was as if buckets were being poured through immense colanders.

Mr Frost was hunting; he returned soaked to the skin and the mare with scratched knees. Under the Captain's directions I made her a steaming bran-mash and Winter and Paul set about drying the poor shivering creature, and bandaging her legs.

By now the lane was eight inches deep in muddy water, and the Captain insisted on taking me home on his motor-bike. We splashed through the floods very slowly as the chain was slipping. In many places streams were flowing across the road and there was a strong current. At Newton we had to give up and the Captain turned home. I splashed my way to Nevis without too much difficulty and had to change all my clothes.

January 6th. It has rained ever since Mother left, but today the clouds rolled back to show a sky of deep, soft blue, and the sun transformed puddles to pools of gold, and raindrops to diamonds.

Everyone had gone to Elworthy Burrows for the gallop, save Paul who had been instructed to take Prudence and Sunstar round to the Martins who were hacking them out. I saddled Conga, and on his return Paul pulled out Punch; we rode up on the hills.

Paul was resplendent in his very best – brown leggings, black boots, tight-fitting jacket and a bowler. Whether in honour of me, or the joy occasioned by the sunshine I don't know but by his almost reverent behaviour I rather think the former.

We rode up Bicknoller Coombe and on to Holford. As we passed the top of the Glen there was a most extraordinary effect – mist lay thick in the hollow and through it tree-tops emerged, looking like the most exquisite lace. Paul remarked that it was as if a veil had been thrown over the valley, an apt description that struck me very much. Just then I saw two black-cock, the first I had seen on the Quantocks.

Instead of riding down Halsway, Paul took me down a little track into Thorncombe, new to me. A loose stone wall runs at its side, with every variety of moss and fern; above this are huge beech trees, their trunks scored with generations of names, and their twisted roots stretching many feet into the bracken. In a deep gully, screened by ferns, a swollen brook rang over pebbles.

From here we joined an old courtyard, grass pushing up between the cobbles. A deserted farm-house flanked it, apple trees pushing against it; Paul said its name is Paradise. The stream bubbles through a pipe into the orchard. Thorncombe House is just beyond; we boldly rode down the back drive and through the stableyard, and after trotting along a lane, came out below Quantock Moor. Conga had behaved himself extremely badly on the hills, bucking and kicking up his heels.

In the afternoon AVS and I went to tea at Hartrow in Besley's car. Besley likes going there; he used to be Harry Sweet Escott's groom, and taking tea in the kitchen is a welcome change from his duties as publican and fish-vendor. But today his car stalled on the first hill and refused to start; we walked on to Stogumber and hired Sully's Maxwell.

We had tea in the dining-room, which I love. It is lofty, with a fine stone arch in the ceiling, dark oak panelling, and a wonderful carved overmantel with figures of saints and quaint patterns.

Mr Sweet Escott is very keen on my hunting with him one day, but at present Peter is poorly; the vet. says his blood is in bad condition.

Returning through a clear starry night we heard distant strains of music – the Watchet Town Band was playing carols below us in Stogumber. Brave and loud it sounded as we drove through; fainter and fainter as we neared home.

January 12th. AVS went to Bristol today, on a mission for Father, who wants a school at Clifton vetted for a client. She is staying tonight with her half-sister. Recently she had a letter from Mrs Webb, to say that they are leaving. The Doctor needs a long holiday, and may decide not to practice again. It is a sad blow, but we are not surprised, as he has been looking worn-out lately. I hear that Nurse was quite hysterical at the news.

The Captain has bought one of Doctor's two old Delage cars, and was setting off in it when I returned from my ride. I had taken Punch up on Staple Hill, and actually got a good gallop out of him. It was one of those days when the clouds are low, blending with the landscape. The big, whale-backed hill above Weacombe loomed against molten sunbeams that turned the valleys to gold, the stream shining in bright strips.

January 14th. A bitter frost yesterday has given place to snow. As I could not ride, I went to Elworthy, and called on Mrs Horsey in her tiny Ashpier cottage. I prayed she would not show me her bad leg. Mercifully, it had healed and she was cheerful. Not that she has much cause, poor soul, for her husband has been ill and off work for a month, the kitchen floor was flooded by the rains, and she has five small children to be fed. I know that farm workers get 30/- a week now – "Ruination, Miss Anne" said Ned – but do they get anything when they are ill?

I had a parcel of books today, among them cousin David Garnett's new novel *The Sailor's Return* – I like it as well as *Lady into Fox,* and better than *The Man at the Zoo.* The wrapper of this American edition describes Tulip, the heroine, as an 'African Negress of High Social Position'. David, who gave it to Father, has underlined this and put three exclamation marks.

January 16th. Heavy snow all the morning, but it is not quite so cold, and when I went up to Brewers Water for a few things it was beginning to thaw, though a few flakes still fell. I hope it clears away so that I can get some more riding before school begins.

AVS has a lovely plan: that she will try to find a cottage hereabouts, to make a permanent home. Then whatever I decide to do if and when I pass the exam., I shall be able to come for holidays. I am delighted – I could not bear to be severed from West Somerset.

We are to move back to Brewers Water on the 20th.

January 23rd. After a ride on the Quantocks with Mr Frost, in a hurricane of wind, I lunched with the Evans Smiths. They want me to take a young girl's part in a play, at an entertainment being got up by Mrs Dalzell. I should have the honour of acting with the Captain – in fact he would be my fiancé! St John Couch and Mrs Dalzell would be the only other actors. I wonder if AVS will allow it?

January 25th. Term begins – just as I am getting excited at signs of Spring. Thrushes sing all day, and the hedges are full of catkins. Bulbs are showing green noses and there is a clump of snowdrops on the bank by the station.

But this morning was far from joyful. I travelled with Miss Ford, who told me it is almost certain that Mr Browne is not coming back. My disappointment told me how much I must have liked him.

January 27th. Today was the first of Canon Yates' lectures. School kindly served me an early lunch and I caught the 2.20 train. The Canon spoke on the Romantic poets, from Burns to Browning. He is a witty speaker and told some amusing anecdotes. AVS, when talking to him afterwards, mentioned Grandpapa Garnett and he said it was the merest chance he had not quoted him in the lecture.

All the local ladies were there but I noted a conspicuous lack of their husbands.

January 29th. A postcard from Mr Sweet Escott has thrown me into the wildest excitement. He will either bring or send Peter for me at 10.15 today for the meet at Bicknoller Post – unless the weather be really bad.

It *was* raining, but not too hard: AVS told me not to count my chickens. I got ready, but it rained harder and harder, and no Peter. I sadly did my prep. – very bitter!

January 30th. After church Mr Sweet Escott asked me to go hunting with him next Saturday. The meet is at Timberscombe so it will mean a hack of fourteen miles; I must be at Hartrow by nine o'clock. I danced for joy all the way home, and am glad now that I did not go yesterday, as now I have a whole week to look forward.

January 31st.   A most exciting ride, the ponies were quite mad. It must be the spring feeling in the air – I saw the first primrose and felt a little mad myself.

There were more thrills when we got back. The Captain was still fighting the new colt he is breaking; by this time it was covered with lather and steaming like a wash-tub. The Captain was sitting on him very quietly, just touching his mouth as light as a feather, and very much on the look-out. The colt was edging towards the wall as if to try and scrape him off.

Getting too near the wall, the Captain dismounted – the colt reared – he dropped his whip, and somehow, the reins. Away went the colt, and scrambled up the dung-heap. We held our breaths, for it drains into an eight foot deep cess-pit, covered with rotten boards.

The Captain shrieked "Whoa-a-a" in a frenzy, the colt steadied himself for a moment and then walked right across the four rotten boards, looking as if about to jump the wall. The Captain swore to great effect, and Paul ran like lightning, stole up to the quivering animal, and got the reins. Then very cautiously he led him back over the pit; as he expressed it afterwards "You could see they boards a-dancing".

We all let out sighs of relief like so many pricked balloons, and the birds began to sing again. Captain re-mounted to resume the fight and we thought it best to withdraw.

As I came down the hill on my way home I heard a blackbird. So clear, so rich – I could have cried for joy. And there he was, on a branch against the sky, the first to sing in 1926.

February 5th.   I awoke to hear rain pouring down. It was still dark, but through the drumming noise I heard a cock crow, and soon light began stealing in. AVS came to call me, as I had to leave for Hartrow at 8.15.

I dressed in growing despair, thinking what a small chance there was of the weather clearing. Mrs Dark came in with my breakfast saying that the rain was stopping, the mist rising, and that it would be a lovely day. So I was persuaded to get ready, and fly off on the chance of it being fine by the time I got to Hartrow.

I hurried to Stogumber. Brewer got the car out in no time and responded to my "Let her rip!"

Arrived at Hartrow, I asked him to wait. Mr Sweet Escott, hearing the maid letting me in, came out napkin under arm and munching his breakfast – "Awfully sorry – fact is I have to stay in – two telegrams expected – I didn't have time to send a message – But look here, if you like to send that fellow back I can give you a decent ride in about an hour's time; stay to lunch and we'll send you home in the pony trap".

The copse at Eastlake. p.8 The bluebell wood

Elworthy from Whites Farm

1

'We walked through the wood in Kensie Lane'

The pump yard, Whites Farm. p.10 'It was like coming home to walk through the courtyard'

p.13 Copse Mead, looking away from Elworthy Combe

p.22 'An early lunch, and then set out for the Quantocks'
(seen from Kensie Lane)

Chap.3 On Hardown Hill, Dorset

Chap.3 Stonebarrow Hill, Dorset   5

p.49 The church at Stogumber

The back 'us fire. p.52 'The wide hearth, black sooty kettle. . . all lit by the leaping flames'

p.56 A reminiscence of Isaac – making rabbit snares

Colwell Farm. p.54 'Green meadows and red ploughed fields'

*A road on the Brendons. p.73 'Turf at the side of
the road planted with double rows of beeches'*

Whites Farm

*Combe Sydenham. p.75 'We walked on and on till we came
to Combe Sydenham'*

I was awfully cut up at no hunting, but as he pointed out, we should not have seen much in the mist. I spent an hour in the morning-room reading old Punches, and at last the horses were ready.

David and I were to ride to Ash Priors with a note. I rode the new grey mare Swallow, and David Peter – the latter very fresh, bucking and rearing. It had cleared up by now and the mist was vanishing; there were patches of blue sky and gleams of sun. Hartrow had snowdrops in the flower beds and the rookery was sheeted with them.

Ash Priors Common

It was a pleasant ride; Ash Priors a straggling village between Bishop's Lydeard and Milverton. Having delivered the note we explored it, and had a gallop on the common, to the dismay of a flock of geese.

We rode home through Lydeard St Lawrence, where David reined up outside the shop and called for two halfpenny buns. Mrs Pullen brought them out on a plate, whereupon he said in a lordly voice "Put them down to Hartrow Manor account" and wheeled Peter round. Mrs Pullen repressed a smile and I burst out laughing.

Riding along a little bridle path we found clumps of primroses blooming on the sheltered bank. It seems years since I last rode those lanes, learning to ride with Mr Sweet Escott on the old mare. Not that he taught me anything but remaining in the saddle!

Lunch was a peculiar meal, as all the boys took turns to argue. David began by asking for some port, and demanding whether there would be enough drink to go round on Tuesday, when there is to be an invitation meet at Hartrow. Then Archer had a long wrangle with our host, and finally, Tod, as to which of the hills at Dunkery is Robin

69

Dawe and which Jenny.

The idea had been that David was to drive me home, but he disappeared soon after lunch so I walked.

I am reading a novel by Sheila Kaye Smith; I like her descriptions of the country, but not of all the women, with 'the scent of her hair', 'her bosom rose and fell' and the inevitable passions and mistaken marriages. The fact is I am sick and tired of *reading* about kisses!

February 9th. About to enter the train this morning, I caught sight of *Mr Browne* in a carriage. Naturally, I was so overcome that I promptly got in, and assuming as calm a manner as possible, enquired after his health.

We talked for a few minutes, then buried ourselves in our newspapers. He had a companion with whom he talked; they only spoke to me to enquire if I minded their smoking. It was not particularly exciting.

The next day he was again travelling, and at Minehead came and talked to me through the window. He seemed shy, and flushed as he spoke, but was very friendly – Miss Ford who has mutual friends, says he is known to be extremely bashful, so I suppose it is a feat to have got to know him at all.

February 11th. I rode to Samford Brett, to collect a subscription for Dr Webb's presentation. Conga was beautifully fresh and trotted briskly, very good till we entered the village, when he started bucking and put a group of school-children to flight.

Samford is a village off the main road, approached by a hollow lane. This widens in the village, with a row of cottages on either side and a stream. Further on it forks, and the two lanes climb a steep green hill. I found the farmer I wanted in a turnip-field, into which I had to lead Conga, and after all that, was told he had already subscribed.

We had the first rehearsal of *In Honour Bound* in the afternoon. Mrs Dalzell is my aunt in this enthralling drama; at one point I have to play her to sleep with the lights turned down – most effective. It is killingly funny rehearsing all this nonsense; we are leaving the caresses till the end.

Of course it was dark by the time we finished and Captain Evans Smith said he would drive me home. The lights of the old Delage grew fainter and fainter; they are functioned by a carbide arrangement on the dash-board. By the time we reached Bustle's cottage they were so dim that the Captain said "Look here Anne, I'm scared to death of these lights, I think I'd better get Bustle to take you".

70

While dear old Bustle was getting ready, the Captain tried to remedy matters so that he could see to drive back. As we bent over there was a sudden blaze and a flame shot up in our faces, illuminating everything for yards around. We both yelled and sprang back – fortunately unhurt. The Captain seized the thing and flung it into a puddle, where it hissed, zizzled, spluttered and died, leaving us in total blackness. I must say I was trembling. It had happened three times before, so was not such a surprise to the Captain, who managed to re-light the lamps to a feeble glimmer. As I love to be frightened, I thoroughly enjoyed the experience.

February 13th. Conga and I held up two large cars today, full of huntsmen in pink coats with their wives and daughters. A large sheep dog had jumped from the hedge and upset him and he was all over the road. Soon after, I heard hounds in full cry and feared I might be carried away in pursuit, but they went off in another direction and all was well.

We then had another exciting incident with the colt, which was being schooled in the top meadow. I had a good time cantering while the Captain knocked a polo ball about.

The colt grew nappy at length and as the Captain dismounted, broke loose and galloped down the steep hill. The Captain yelled "The GATE, Anne!" – I had no need to touch Conga, who was off like the wind.

But we were a moment too late, and the precious, beautiful colt, who is to be worth £500 when he is finished, was tearing to what seemed inevitable destruction at the closed gate. Conga was flying down the hill at break-neck speed with me lying back in the saddle, my head nearly on his tail. I had never galloped downhill before and was terrified.

Fortunately we had not latched the gate; the colt pushed it open and gained the lane. We soon caught him where he stood trembling and panting. The Captain mounted with set mouth and rode off to battle, telling me I had better go home, and by his expression I thought perhaps I had! He told me afterwards that he had never seen anything so funny as Conga flying down that hill with me tugging as hard as I could. Had he not been so anxious about the colt he would have stood and roared. Heartless man!

As I was crossing the stable yard Filbert leant from his box and gave a vicious bite in my shoulder. It was extremely painful and brought tears to my eyes but the others thought it very funny. Mr Frost cheerfully said that I should not be able to go to any dances, as I shall bear purple tooth-marks to the end of my days.

71

February 15th. In the afternoon the Webbs came to say goodbye, Mrs Webb flying in to say they could not stop and would we come out – her husband was just driving up from the station.

So we went out; he stopped beside us, we laughed and talked and shook hands. It was not till my hand was in his and I looked into his eyes that I realised how sad he was to go, and how I felt. It took all the sunshine away for a moment. Then Mrs Webb got into the car and with a hum and a whirr they were out of sight, and so out of our lives. Horrible.

February 19th. Mr Frost was nearly killed today by the mad brown mare, Gladwys. They were hunting and she tried to jump the deep gully – at least thirteen feet wide – in Bicknoller Combe. Mr Frost shot over her neck and landed on his head on the opposite bank; Gladwys too landed on her head, all four legs in the air and her face deep in the mud. She was not at all hurt and gave him a very lively hack home.

I was just changing for lunch at Brewers Water when I heard hounds, and running to the window saw the pack streaming across the plough below our home meadow. I rushed down in time to open the yard gate to a large field, headed as usual by Peggy and Joan Kershaw. They do ride hard! Major Storey and Skipper came next; they all strained through, a mass of pricked ears and snorting nostrils, each rider touching his hat and thanking me. Soon all the hurry, creak of leather and chink of iron had gone, and nothing remained but the smell of hot horses and the trodden turf and mud.

February 22nd. Miss Ford told me of great goings-on at Taunton yesterday. J.H. Thomas came down, to be met at the station by hundreds of railway-men – he used to be a stoker on the GWR. They were led by Sparks, the handsome golden-haired young Labour candidate who is our signalman at Dunster.* They all marched in procession to the War Memorial where Thomas laid a wreath and he and Sparks spoke.

Then to St Andrews where they held a men's service, Thomas reading the lessons. In the evening there was a meeting at the Lyceum Theatre, Sparks being Chairman. That boy is coming on – he will be Prime Minister one day, and I shall be able to tell how he used to open our carriage door: "All tickets please" and smile at Miss Ford's "We're all shareholders today, Mr Sparks. – Such a handsome boy, my dears."

---

* He stood as candidate for Taunton in 1929, and for Acton as the 1st candidate put up by the West Country.

CHAPTER VII

February 25th – May 2nd, 1926

❊❊❊ ❊❊❊

*F*EBRUARY 25th.   I was able to pick a large bunch of primroses
today; the flowers are coming out fast. There are daisies and
celandines everywhere and chaffinches and thrushes sing all day long.
I leant over the gate in the lane for a long time this evening watching
the sun dip down; the down-train glided below me, its sound
deadened by the deep cutting but the steam rising to catch the
crimson light. At last the glow faded, the moon rose, and I stayed on
listening to the sweet, sweet birds.

March 6th.   Actually a fine day for a long ride with Mr Sweet Escott.
He sent the stable-boy down for me with Peter and Swallow; I hacked
Peter up to Hartrow as Swallow had to be shod, and sat in the drawing
room talking to Mrs Sweet Escott till Swallow returned.

We set off at a brisk pace as Mr Sweet Escott had to be home by two
o'clock. It seemed a long time since I had been up Elworthy Burrows
and I thoroughly enjoyed it. Our conversation was of farming, horses
and hunting, and the country.

We were soon on the top of the Brendon Hills and trotting past
Raleigh's Cross; we cantered on green turf at the side of the road,
planted with double rows of beeches on stone banks. Isaac once told
me that his grandfather was among those employed to make these
banks, and to plant the saplings. It was at the time of the Enclosure
Acts and they were paid 6d a week.

Here and there the beeches had been cut and we could see – for
miles – huge sweeps of bleak hill country, swelling ridges of bracken
and heather. And, pointing black fingers, the shafts of the old iron-
ore mines.

We rode on and on, over ridge and fell, the wind full in our faces
and smelling of the sea. Mr Sweet Escott pointed out landmarks and
told me the names of all we passed. One point of interest was The
Naked Boy, a large white stone at the side of the road. It does
resemble a figure, especially at dusk I expect.

The desolation of these hills is remarkable. Occasionally one sees an old grey cottage or farmhouse half hidden in a hollow, but the only living things are hill sheep, carrion crows and hawks. We met three people the entire time.

At the furthest edge of the Brendons we reined up for the view. There was the sea, angry and grey with white horses racing in Porlock Bay. There was Bossington Point, and there Exmoor stretching away. Behind us the Quantocks were in brilliant sunshine, blue shadows chasing along them, like hills in a vivid dream.

We trotted all the way home but even so it was 2.30. We had done twenty miles.

March 8th. It was a surprise to hear today that Paul is leaving the stables. On hearing that he had been riding his motor-bike the Captain gave him a month's notice. He has enlisted in the Guards and joins his regiment today. They parted in a very friendly manner. Paul, hanging his head, said he was "very sorry for all he had done wrong" and the Captain patted his back and gave him advice on the perils and snares of army life.

March 10th. Uncle Arthur arrived today. He has cycled all the way from Sussex. It is lovely to have him – exactly the same. Three Tasmanian friends of his are expected soon; AVS has found them lodgings while Uncle Arthur stays with us.

March 14th. Uncle Arthur and I spent the whole of a perfect day on the Quantocks. Taking a plentiful supply of sandwiches, we set off about 11.0 a.m. and climbed Bicknoller Combe. As we walked over the top to Holford larks soared up all round us, singing loudly as they climbed into the sky. A fresh breeze was blowing, and all round stetched moorland, fields, woods and hills; here and there the gleam of water.

We found a track leading down into the Glen, it reminded me of Tom's descent in *The Water Babies,* for it was just as steep and with the same sparkling stream below.

A little path led through a narrow valley – fresh green grass at first, then an oak-wood. The brook now flowed through a steep, rocky gorge, with big falls and deep brown pools, the rocks covered with mosses and ferns. We lunched in this glen, sitting on rocks overhanging the dancing water, and afterwards dozed.

Following up the stream we found the gorge more and more rocky and precipitous. It was a long climb but at last we came out of the woods to bare heath. A track led us to the old carriage-way, where to our surprise we met three very smart young men. Uncle Arthur remarked that though we had not seen any deer, we had had the unexpected sight of sky-blue Oxford bags.

At Triscombe we descended and had a large tea at the Blue Ball Inn, where Mrs Hayes' step-mother, the landlady, was surprised and delighted to see us.

March 15th. Uncle Arthur and I went out to pick primroses in the afternoon, and the lane I had selected off Ashpier proved to the one place without any. So we walked on and on till we came to Combe Sydenham, and thought we might as well go into Pond Woods. I had a private reason for wishing to go there, as I had suggested it before starting. AVS had poured cold water on the idea, saying we could not possibly get so far. And here we were, with the sound of the stream below us, the placid levels of the ponds reflecting the height upon height of trees, the clumps of pale primroses and the sappy green dog-mercury. I told Ned's story of the devil being exorcised with Bell Book and Candle from Combe Sydenham Manor, and how he was thrown, under the guise of a black dog, into the fifth pond. The boy carrying Satan in a sack was told by the Bishop in charge not to look back. But of course he did, to see the pond a flaming mass of brimstone. "And" added Ned "thik there pond 'ave been stone-dry ever since." Which is true.

March 17th. We all (the three Tasmanian ladies whose name is Dunbabin) AVS, Uncle Arthur, and I set out for Elworthy, the eldest Miss Dunbabin and AVS in a car up Ashpier. We met at the top of Mondsborough and proceeded through Elworthy looking as Uncle Arthur said like a Cook's Tour.

Mrs Hayes gave us a hearty welcome, but was rather overpowered at first. Gordon and I ran about feeding fowls and collecting the eggs till tea was ready; by then the ice was broken and Mrs Hayes much interested in hearing about Tasmanian farming.

After a royal tea we went out to look for Ned; he was loading mangolds in Five Acres. We walked by the cart, helping to unload for the cows in the pasture-fields. A solitary huntsman came slowly down Hill Road – Major Storey. He did not recognise me with a pitch-fork in my hand, and rode on evidently struggling to identify me. After him lolloped two enormous and exhausted stag-hounds.

Ned had tea when we got in, and a good farming chat, after which we took leave for our long walk home.

March 23rd. An idea has been growing that I might go to an Art School when I leave Minehead. Miss Hammet suggested it and the family seem to approve – except Rayne. She writes that she hopes I will not decide on it, as a true artist should be willing to starve in a garret – and if he did sell any pictures it would only prove them bad ones!

As I am fond of drawing horses Miss Hammet suggests my taking lessons with a Captain Brandling at Minehead, who is a good animal artist and teaches well. AVS has written for the parents' consent.

As we were at breakfast it began to snow heavily with enormous flakes. It has been very cold for the last few days, but we were not prepared for this.

I was in hopes that it would delay Uncle Arthur's departure today, as the ground was soon white. He came to the station to say goodbye, but missed the chance as he was still teasing Miss Smith [a regular fellow passenger of mine] about her Scots accent when the train went out. He gave me 10/- last night, bless him; I am going to buy another de la Mare, *The Listeners,* and the 1913-15 *Georgian Poetry.*

It was melancholy returning from school to find no kind uncle on the platform. Every day he came to meet me and escorted me down in the mornings. I shall miss him terribly.

March 29th. My first lesson with Capt. Brandling. He is a typical soldier and you know at once that you will get on well if you talk of sport in any form. He set me to draw a horse, out of my head, in charcoal. My first attempt had to be rubbed out, but with a few hints I achieved a fairly good stationary animal. I am to go again on Wednesday and think I shall learn a great deal.

April 2nd. I have been feeling poorly all the week; AVS and I have both had bad colds and she is still looking like a ghost. However, we were well enough to go to church, it being Good Friday.

In the afternoon I went into the wood to pick primroses for the Easter Church decorations; the ground was yellow with them and the whole wood smelt sweet – and a high wind made music in the tree-tops. Stooping over the flowers made me dizzy, so that everything grew blurred. I sat down, listening to the almost organ-music above, and feeling harrowed by the events of Good Friday. The whole thing is too deep; I can't realise or understand why it should have had to be so.

April 3rd. Today was the dress-rehearsal of *In Honour Bound* and Miss Webster is coming for the weekend to see it. I rode in the morning – I have not been on a horse for a fortnight. Mrs Evans Smith was rushing between stable yard and the Dalzell's barn where we are to act. It is large and a good stage has been erected. We had a fine ride, over the part of the Quantocks badly burnt last week; it was while Uncle Arthur was here. We went out to see flames rushing along the top of the hills, most exciting. The newspapers all had accounts of it – even the *Mail*.

Miss Webster came by the two o'clock train, very tired as she had been up at crack of dawn to watch a motor-rally on Porlock Hill. So we rested all the afternoon. Having changed my underclothes so that I should not reveal a vest beneath my low-necked frock, we walked to Bicknoller through the dusk. A maid showed me up to the bathroom at the Dalzells, and brought me my dress. Mrs Dalzell lent me a pink satin wrap – it is to have a white fox-fur collar for the performance – and a lace and mother of pearl fan.

Then she made us all up, with many delays and last touches to our attire. Although we had quite a large audience, all the servants and a few friends, I was not nervous and actually did not mind playing my piece on the piano, which I had been dreading.

We did it through twice and then walked home through the dark. I was too excited to get to sleep, but Miss Webster did so at once.

April 5th. Miss Webster and I had our breakfast in bed, and I regret to say lay laughing and ragging till eleven. After lunch we went by train to watch the first day of Polo. We found that Mr Frost was playing; his girl-friend the little Nurse was there with his mother. AVS sat in their dicky and Miss Webster and I in the Evans Smiths'.

The colt was playing for the first time, and although very green and making some mistakes, was all that we hoped, keeping beautifully balanced. It is easy to see he will be a tip-top pony.

Although it was hot and bright, wisps of mist came up from the sea and enfolded the hills, the castle rising through it. Now and then the players were transformed into phantoms wheeling and turning as if in the mists of a dream.

April 9th. The great day of the Entertainment. It was all most exciting. The Captain had a violent sick headache and had to be dosed with everything from aspirin to whisky. There seemed a great many of us females dressing, as there were two other sketches besides *In Honour Bound*; we had a bedroom which was soon resounding to shrieks of laughter and general excitement.

The barn was packed, and as we waited in the wings and heard the hum from the audience I did feel scared and shivery. But as soon as we went on I forgot all about that and thoroughly enjoyed it – the sea of pink oval faces staring up, and the ripples of laughter. It was a spendid audience, even laughing at my "Lovely young man with *such* a sweet moustache". I was even a little disappointed when the orchestra took over to such effect that my piano-playing was drowned.

Everyone acted well. The Captain forgot his headache, and St John and I were carried away sufficiently to embrace each other which we could never manage at rehearsals. At the end, when my fiancé kisses me, I regret to say that my complexion was ruined by a large red smudge.

After the splendid applause and curtain I rushed away to change, and then sat in the front row, leaning on Peggy Kershaw to watch 'Betsy Bates' and 'Our New Butler', which were very well received, as were Mr Moger's comic songs.

When the final curtain fell Dreda (St John's sister) and I climbed on stage and went to the Dalzells', where we found the dining-room crowded. A table was laden with jellies, trifles, sandwiches, claret cup and lemonade. I talked to Dorothy Dalzell and Dreda for the most part, but the Captain came round to chat, and kindly offered to remove my make-up. We retired to the bathroom, where he was most charming and complimentary.

All too soon Barber, the Dalzell's chauffeur, came round with the car to take us home. I climbed into bed with the pleasant thought that it would all happen again tomorrow.

April 10th. A perfect day, the sun streaming from a cloudless sky, the birds shouting, and dew sparkling on the meadows. And the flowers in Kensie Lane; masses of primroses, dog violets and daisies everywhere; hedges and trees are all softened with buds and young leaf. The Archers were chatting in the road at Bicknoller as I passed, and shouted "Congratulations on last night!"

The ponies were saddled up, Mildmay for me, Marco for Mr Frost and the colt for the Captain. I was pleased to have my sweet gentle Milly again, the pretty dear. We went to a field where Mr Frost played polo, the Captain schooled the colt and I tried to school Milly, actually succeeding in getting her to passage.

Then we returned to change the men's mounts for Kim and Duncan, and while we were re-saddling we heard the hunting-horn and blobs of pink came up the lane. In trotted Charlie Back and the whip, the entire pack drifting at their feet, come to see the puppies. We called and yelled, but to no purpose, and we remembered that they were out with Winter, exercising.

At length they departed, and we set out and to my joy, were told to shorten our stirrups as we were to gallop.

78

We rode jockey-wise, perched on our horses' withers. Mildmay was as keen as mustard, and as soon as we lined up to start and the Captain said "Right", was off like an arrow.

We did not gallop fast, but at a fine, even pace, Milly well in front all the time. I found it difficult to keep her in at first, but we had three gallops and I kept her well controlled for the last, and was praised. I can't imagine anything lovelier than galloping like this – the speed of it, the joy of seeing the daisies sliding away under you, the feel of the pony's smooth neck between your hands, the way she takes hold of the bit, the smooth even motion, and the thudding of hoofs on the turf.

The Captain was in a very jovial mood, teasing me about my performance last night and how he had kissed me, etc., which of course, I thoroughly enjoyed.

I helped Mrs Evans Smith get lunch, and while she took a rest, washed the dishes from breakfast and our meal. The Captain meanwhile sat down at the piano and played for an hour, extemporarily and sometimes rather beautifully. I had no idea he could play so well. Then I curled up on their bed and must have slept for an hour, as I was awakened by the Captain at the window. He gave me a note left by his wife, to tell me to go to the barn where I was wanted to decorate programmes.

The Captain was incorrigible at tea, but we got away somehow to the barn, where we found St John wandering in a boiled shirt and dress trousers, looking for things lost last night. I was of course still in riding clothes, and went to the bathroom to wash and change. As before, Mrs Dalzell made us up; I was feeling 'depressed and out of sorts' to quote the play, but a timely draught of port put that right.

The house was crammed again, but tonight the audience was chiefly of villagers, who liked the farces best. The Captain brought the house down as 'Our New Butler' and at the end was presented with an enormous bottle of Bass and a huge corkscrew. We ladies had boxes of chocolates and Mrs Dalzell a bouquet.

I kept on my pink frock and wrap this time as I had only breeches to change into, but the party only consisted of the cast and AVS. However, St John and the Captain were very kind about my acting, and when the latter was cleaning off my make-up he said he honestly thought the whole show had been a success.

What a pity it is all over! I have enjoyed not only the compliments and fun, but getting to know people better, and to feel that they like me in return. I hardly knew Dreda or Mrs Dalzell before, and they are so nice. Mrs Dalzell had taken to calling me 'Kid'.

April 12th.   AVS had been to the vicarage at Bicknoller recently, and had invited Dreda and St John to tea today. Dreda is a clever girl, about twenty-one; she is very jolly and unaffected, studying at Exeter for her teacher's Diploma.

She told us about her work and was interesting in describing the weeks she spends teaching at various elementary schools. We were deep in a discussion on modern poets and authors when St John arrived, and joined in, displaying good taste and not a little knowledge of the subject.

We had a grand tea about six. St John ate heartily, still talking of books. He said if he were asked to name the five best poems in the English language he would choose *Lycidas,* Keats' *Ode to Autumn,* Hood's *Bridge of Sighs,* Swinburne's *Prospice* and Byron's *Isles of Greece.* I thought the Hood rather a queer choice for a boy of twenty, but agreed with the rest.

As we walked a little way back with our guests a red glow of sunset still burned through the dusk, the air smelt of flowers and dew, and bats were flitting through a sky where stars were already trembling. When we turned to go in the sickle moon lifted herself clear of the tree tops and shone pale in the ashes of the western fire.

April 14th.   We spent the morning packing all our possessions, as Mrs Dark has given AVS notice again, and this time has not rescinded it. So AVS has had to sally forth and engage fresh rooms. On our return from our visits – I am going to stay with Helen at Sittingbourne – we are to live at Manor Farm in Stogumber. It will be quite a walk to the station, and further from Bicknoller, otherwise it seems nice.

April 15th.   Genius was run over today while we were out; she ran right under a large red car that had slowed down for us. Mr Frost let out a stream of abuse at the unfortunate driver, for which I apologised as 'Duddles' galloped after Genius. The poor man was quite speechless and his wife pained and shocked. Fortunately Mr Frost returned and apologised for his language himself.

Genius howled himself into a field but soon came limping back; we went straight home and telephoned the Hunt Kennels from the Post Office. But Charlie was at the Dulverton Point to Point, and so was the vet. So we made the poor hound as comfortable as we could; he came out and hobbled round the yard. It seemed as if a hind leg is out of joint; I doubt if he will be any good for hunting.

Helen has written to me about Sittingbourne, where her father is doing duty for the vicar. She says it is nothing but slums and chimneys and a poor exchange for the delights of hills and sea at Hardown. But

I am sure I shall enjoy the visit and it will be all new country to me.

April 16th. It was raining cats and dogs when I woke, and went on for the whole of my journey. We had an hour to wait at Taunton and then had to travel in different parts of the train, as AVS going to Southampton was in a coach slipped off at Westbury.

My carriage was full, but I had a corner seat, and amused myself by watching raindrops spattering the window and blurring the view of fields and woods as they flashed by. A bevy of school-girls rushing up and down the corridor were so exactly like those in *Girls Own Annuals* and the works of Angela Brazil that I was quite fascinated.

Dicky was to meet me at Paddington to take me to Victoria; I waited for what seemed an age in a seething crowd of porters, frenzied ladies, wailing babies, and hurried men, till I began to think myself forgotten. Just as I had given up hope, I saw his broad face. He drove me to Victoria in the Baby Austin and we lunched at a buffet, when he had to hurry away.

I had to wait for my train but at last it came in and was soon gliding through London.

The streets went on and on till I began to think they stretched all the way to Sittingbourne. In the end we were out into undulating country where acres of orchards in bloom alternated with hopfields.

Helen met me and took me to the Vicarage, a pleasant, large house next the church. There certainly *are* chimneys in Sittingbourne, and I should not call it an ideal town, but it is not as bad as Helen led me to expect. There is a large paper factory, said to be the biggest in the world, and brick-works, but these are empty owing to a strike.

Both Mr and Mrs Marsden are here; the latter is very much of an invalid, sweet, frail and daintily amusing. I can't make my host out as yet; he is as silent as the grave and betrays no interest in anything save the Church and Gilbert and Sullivan. The result is a trifle damping to general conversation.

After tea Helen and I went a short stroll to take the rattle of trains from my head. We went along streets of the Nottingham lace curtain, aspidistra, mangy cat variety till we came to a public garden. Beyond this the houses ended in cherry-orchards, covered with snow-white blossom, above the greenest grass I have ever seen.

Beyond the orchards stretches a broad, level belt of country, cultivated for the most part for hops. Here and there, over the rise of a low hill, peer the conical tops of oast-houses, or the red roofs of farms. The farms have tiled roofs stained with lichen and moss. Chiefly built of mellow red brick, some have lathe and plaster walls with old, old beams.

April 17th. Mrs Marsden took us to Canterbury today. As soon as we left the station we entered a shady park, bounded by the old city wall; flint stones in mortar. We walked along this wall, looking across the moat, now filled with grass, trees and flowers, to the roofs of that part of the town now outside the walls. Every few yards there is a turret with arrow slits, and I suppose where we walked, with children and nurses sunning themselves, there were once sentries tramping up and down and manning the turrets.

Coming down from the ramparts on the other side of the park, we found ourselves on a raised path above the market. We looked down on a seething crowd of farmers and farmers' boys, flocks of panting sheep wedged into pens, the broad backs of cows and bullocks, and patient, shiny-coated cart horses. Men poked them with sticks and examined their wool, hooves, and teeth, and a hot, fat auctioneer in a white coat shouted their merits in a voice easily heard above all the din.

We watched this lively scene for some time, and then gained the High Street. It is a narrow winding street with houses new and old elbowing each other and all crowding onto the pavement. There were crowds of people too, farmers and their wives, smartly dressed girls and boys, tradespeople, and the County arriving in their Daimlers and Armstrong-Siddeleys for shopping.

Farmers and their wives

Suddenly across a little side street we saw an old grey arch; through it and towering above were the towers and pinnacles of the Cathedral. Once through the arch the bustle, cries, and colours of the High Street faded; we only saw the emerald turf and old trees of the Close, and immediately before us, the Cathedral towering up in one great harmonious whole.

In another moment we were inside, and just as the High Street had fallen back from the Close, so now the light and colour of the day disappeared and we were in an awed dimness. Around us pillars, dizzy in their height, rose up and up to support the sculptured roof. But that was so high that a mist seemed to float beneath it. Below the pillars windows glowed like precious stones, of all colours, and of such intensity that I felt I had never seen pure colour before. The coolness and dusk wrapped us closely; there was a cold, salty smell like the wet stones of a beach. Footsteps echoed on and on like the distant roar of the sea, or wind in a pine forest.

We went round, admiring quaint carvings, figures of soldiers, angels and saints, knights on tombs, and the wonderful tomb of the Black Prince, his armour hanging above it. And St Augustine's Chair, and of course the actual stone where St Thomas was assassinated, which has a black border.

Then we went into a cloister and sitting on a low wall looked out between the arches. Old red roofs and tumble-down chimneys peered down on one side at a stretch of green turf.

Last of all we visited the Kent War Memorial. This we found at the end of the Close where an arch led to a square garden. The old brick walls were covered with blooming fruit trees and wallflowers; under them a wide bed was planted with old fashioned flowers. A large square lawn had old, gnarled trees; an apple or two, a quince, a pear, and a walnut. The apple trees were covered with pink and white blossom that every puff of wind scattered on the lawn. A broad stone walk crossed the grass, meeting in the centre at the memorial bearing the names of the men of Kent killed in the War.

We sat long on a bench enjoying the sunshine and the flowers. Presently an old, bent man in a black gown came to talk, and told us he was from North Devon. He said the garden had been the monk's bowling green, and that they had kept their bee-hives in the curious arches we had noticed in the walls.

After lunch in a restaurant we went to see the Canterbury Theatrical Society's production of *Utopia Ltd*. It was almost as good as D'Oyly Carte. This makes the fourth Gilbert & Sullivan I have seen; I still like *Ruddigore* best.

We had our tea at a wonderful place called Binks. It looked so exclusive and select that at first we feared we had entered a gentlemen's club, especially as the only occupants were three men smoking in a corner. Then we had a rush for our train. After hurrying though the town we arrived at the station just as the guard was about to blow his whistle.

Mrs Marsden and I threw ourselves into a first class carriage and the train steamed out. As Helen had been ahead of us, we surmised that she must have got in too, but she did not appear at any of the stations we stopped at, and as she had no money we began to worry lest she had been left behind.* However, she alighted at Sittingbourne. Her mother was quite exhausted by all the sight-seeing and the rush for our train, and went immediately to bed.

* Their coach was divided into compartments, with no corridor.

April 18th. Helen and I went to the eight o'clock service, and a country walk after breakfast. We found our way through the snowy orchards – everyone is allowed this joy all the year as fruit is too abundant to be worth stealing – and past attractive old farms, till we cast anchor in a sunny field where we lay on a heap of golden wheat straw. Here we were blissfully content, chewing straws, our backs against a rick, dozing, and discussing life. Helen still talks of Bob Coombes and wonders if he will be in Dorset this summer.

We took another lazy walk in the afternoon, though a large hopfield. I found this fascinating, as whichever way you looked, you faced a straight line of poles. Coming to a large chalk pit, we sat on its edge, sheltered by a thick blackthorn hedge covered with blossom, so that before and behind there was dazzling whiteness. There was nothing else but the vast sky and its clouds, also dazzling white.

I enjoyed the service at church in the evening, because the sermon was the only one I have heard in which the preacher said exactly what I would have liked to say. Every time I thought 'Oh, I do hope he says so-and-so' or 'That is what I think, but why doesn't he emphasise it?' Mr Marsden promptly did so. And at supper he talked a good deal and I was emboldened to talk too; we had quite a long discussion. After supper he played and sang from several Gilbert & Sullivan operas.

April 19th. We spent today at Sheerness-on-Sea, which I thought a queer place. The station is surrounded by poky little houses, each with its washing in a back yard. A bare space like a rubbish dump, though a few flower beds surrounded the station, led to the esplanade, which like all esplanades, was broad and made of asphalt. Against this a grey sea lipped soundlessly. We walked on and on, past the houses, factories, shops, hard tennis courts, and public gardens, and at last came to the end. The asphalt merged into a road, and the houses straggled into weedy fields and then stopped.

We stopped too, and lay on a narrow strip of shingle with our backs against a breakwater. There was an ominous calm over everthing; the oily sea, the town, the dim coastline over the water; everything was silent. An unearthly pale sunlight filtered through leaden clouds, warming us as we dozed. Now and then guns at Chatham boomed sleepily.

Something made me sit up suddenly, and I saw that the sky behind us was now inky black. Ripples scudded over the sea, no longer grey but a deep blue-green. Then a terrific clap of thunder rolled across the sky and died away, muttering. We hurried back down the esplanade as fast as we could, but we were hurrying into the storm, not away from it. The sea behind us was still calm, but before us was shot with the most wonderful peacock-green lights under a black sky.

It soon began to rain and by the time we reached the first shelter the storm was over. We dried off while eating our lunch in a somewhat comfortless manner, had tea in the town, and then went to a cinema.

We saw Douglas Fairbanks in *Don Q*. It was quite good, and we laughed till we cried at some of the comic films that preceded it.

Poor Mrs Marsden is still in bed and seems likely to remain so.

April 22nd.   Helen and I went to tea at the other Sittingbourne Vicarage today, where we met a great many people. Our cheerful host and hostess were genial, small and tubby, both with rosy faces like the Cheeryble brothers.* Besides them and their fifteen year old daughter there was a brother of the vicar, with his four children aged between fifteen and twenty-three; another parson with wife and two little boys, and one other man. So we sat down fifteen to tea and were merry; Mrs Cheeryble did not seem to think the number at all out of the way.

The thunder last Monday broke up the weather to such an extent that we have hardly gone out save for visits to the butcher, the baker, and the candlestick maker. But this evening, after a 'high tea', Helen and I again went to the cinema, to see a Zane Grey film *The Thundering Herd*. The scenery was of Yellowstone Park and there were studies of bison grazing and stampeding, and of Red Indians. The story of course was as thrilling as possible, and gave us palpitations as good scenarios should. Altogether a highly successful entertainment.

April 24th.   After saying goodbye to my host and hostess – the latter still upstairs, I left for London this morning.

AVS met my train and we proceeded to Highgate by 'bus and tram. Miss Love was alone at West Hill – such a beautifully clean No. 26 under her care. She keeps the house in apple-pie order, the furniture so well polished that one can see one's face in the table-tops. There are flowers in the rooms and even the dreadful old bath is spotless. How different from the dingy, servantless years of the war! Sad to say, Mother is away.

April 25th.   I gave AVS a little manicure set for her birthday. Father and I went the usual Sunday stroll over Parliament Hill Fields, very gay at this time of the year with people enjoying themselves in brightly coloured clothes, and the trees and bushes as yet free of soot.

* In Dickens' *Nicholas Nickleby*

A young lady, Miss Cumston, came in the afternoon to discuss books with Father, [she designed a jacket for one of his books] and I was expecting Rex. He came while I was getting tea in the basement, and said "You will come to a show with me, Anne?" Of course I needed no persuasion, and we looked at possible plays in the newspaper. *Katya the Dancer* was chosen; we are to go on Tuesday if Rex can get tickets.

April 26th. AVS and I spent the morning shortening my frock and petticoat for tomorrow night. Also we had to remove a quantity of grease-paint. Mrs Dalzell had lavishly spread it on the neck as well as on me – I am thankful to say that it came off with petrol. Fancy my going out to dinner and the theatre with a young man!

Father, Dicky, and I spent a peaceful evening reading in the study; I am deep in *Kenilworth,* my holiday task, and at long last find that I can enjoy Walter Scott. I do like the study, especially at night. The book-lined walls look mellow in the lamp-light, row on row of stolid old chaps in dark leather coats, enlivened here and there by a gay youngster in crimson, blue, or green. And I like the mantelpiece, cluttered with pipes, miniatures, pictures of Dumas*, and the Rossetti clock ticking solemnly in the centre. Grandpapa smiles benignly down on the chaos, for not only are the walls completely covered with books, but there are books on the table, the sofa, and in corners, on the floor.

I can well believe Father's story of how he overheard two girls walking up the hill when our lamp was lit but the curtains undrawn: "Why, Ivy – I didn't know the public library 'ad been moved up 'ere"!

April 27th. Helen came in on her way back to school from Sittingbourne and took tea with us; she says that her mother is at last better. She sat with me while I dressed for the evening out – most envious, and interested in every particular.

At 5.45 I departed to meet Rex at the office. A horrible youth admitted me, and on hearing my name remarked that he thought he saw a likeness, much to my disgust. I don't think I am as much like Father or Dicky as all that. But perhaps he meant it as a compliment, thinking it an honour to resemble the senior partner.

I waited fifteen long minutes for Rex, in Father's very comfortable room. He arrived breathless and apologetic, in dress clothes, and carrying an opera hat. We departed in haste, taking a taxi to

* Robert was an authority on Dumas *père et fils.* His Dumas collection was bequeathed to Mr F.W. Reed in New Zealand and is now housed in that country.

Frasconi's restaurant.

It was a sort of Aladdin's palace, all gilt and roses, with pillars supporting glass domes and golden roofs, while at every turn one saw one's reflection in enormous mirrors.

And the dinner! Rex was tired and quiet at first, as he had had to fly up to Hornsey Lane after a lecture, fling on his clothes – which took three minutes – and fly down again. And he hates a rush, but the dinner soon put that right. He ordered asparagus, which I have never had, and to my distress proceeded to eat it in his fingers! On looking into various mirrors I was reassured by the reflections of other diners doing the same and so bravely tackled my own. It was delicious.*

We had wine to drink, and coffee and a liqueur afterwards, not to mention a cocktail for Rex first. I refused this, as I felt quite excited enough as it was. As the meal wore on we became increasingly pleased with life and ourselves; Rex seemed delighted with me and paid me some very nice compliments.

We had a taxi to Daly's theatre and were shown to our seats in the fourth row of the stalls. Leslie Henson was at his best, and to our delight a song we all had on the brain last Autumn was encored again and again: 'Leander, my dear goosey-gander'.

Rex took another taxi home so we could talk undisturbed. We made a solemn vow to tell one another the instant either of us fell in love, and to be good friends all our lives. The taxi was dismissed at the bottom of West Hill, to avoid undue interest from our elders. And before we had walked far Dicky overtook us, pushing his bicycle, returning from having supper with friends.

West Hill

We found Father and AVS sitting up for us, and sipped hot milk, chatting about the show till Rex left and I went to bed.

April 30th. AVS went off early this morning to see her mother at Folkestone. It was a foggy, disagreeable day and I stayed in, reading *The Lives of the Rakes,*† a new acquisition of Father's, in three

* Later, the asparagus bed was an important feature of Anne's garden.

† by Edwin Beresford Chancellor, published in 6 volumes in 1924 & 25

volumes. They make entertaining reading, but what beasts those men were! In the brief piece I read about the Prince Regent he seduced seven women, well before his affair with Lady Fitzherbert.

After a solitary tea I went for a walk. Rain had cleared the fog and a blue-grey mist was drifting in long trails between the trees. I had the fields to myself save for a couple in Millfield Lane. They were seated on a log, their arms round each other, most gloriously drunk and singing happily. So weird they looked, two bedraggled mortals holding on to one another while the damp leaves dripped upon them, enwrapped in waves of mist.

May 1st. It was not a good May-day, being cold and still foggy. I went up to the Grove School to fetch Helen, who was to come to tea and meet Rex. She took me over the school, first to No. 2 to see some newly re-decorated bedrooms. Miss Fletcher was hanging pictures in the dining room and appeared graciously pleased to see me; I was told that I must join the OGA when I leave Llanberis [the Minehead school].

We walked across the gardens to Grove Bank and went to the Library. It was the first time I have entered it except on Break-up and OG Day, as we were not allowed in until we were sixteen. It is hard to realise how we have grown up, as we are all relatively still the same height. It was only when I caught sight of little girls, or some familiar object that I used to look up at, that I could realise my status.

At the Art room, The Cubes, I was shown frescoes on the walls. The paper has been stripped and the girls have painted some splendid scenes. A large one over the fireplace of St George and the Dragon was done by Helen, and her friend Drusilla has painted Queen Elizabeth and her courtiers at one end of the room, and a spirited Boadicea in her chariot at the other.

We called on Miss Lacey, who, of all things, has had her hair Eton-cropped! Apart from this startling change she appeared exactly the same, even to her crooked black tie. She talked of her visit to France, the prospect of a general strike, and the school, while we sat and made intelligent noises.

We then had to run down West Hill, as Father had invited people to tea. Arriving breathless, we found that Rex and Miss Cumston had already come. Miss Cumston is sister to the pretty girl who came last week; she is as attractive and nice as her sister, but dark instead of fair.

We all went for walks after tea, Father escorting his guest – his other did not turn up – and I with Helen and Rex. Coming back, when I mentioned our return to Somerset next week Rex was dismayed and said he had not realised it was to be so soon. He would like to come to

Stogumber in the summer.

They all stayed to dinner, after which Dicky took Miss Cumston home on his way to a party, and we played Raging Demons. Rex and I then escorted Helen back to school, and coming home he invited me out to dinner again on Monday, and a cinema.

All things have to end, and walking down West Hill under the stars, with the lights painting the trees with weird colour and velvet shadows, could not last forever. But I went to bed very happy.

May 2nd. Oh, lack-a-day! Dicky unfolded the *Observer* at breakfast, and in big black headlines it said 'General Strike arranged for Tuesday'. The news seemed to get up on end and hit me. Of course I've known that the Government and the Trades Union have been trying to reach a settlement for days, but I had taken for granted that they would find one.

AVS thought the best thing we could do was to return to Somerset tomorrow, as there may be no trains on Tuesday. For once I was loth to leave London, as Rex has invited me out to dinner on Monday, and urged running the risk. In the midst of discussion Helen appeared. She had come to ask me to go with her to Westminster Abbey, as there was a service with special music. However, AVS vetoed this, as we are going to see Miss Rossetti after lunch.

While Helen helped me to make my bed, I conceived the brilliant idea of writing a note to Rex, telling him of our departure, and asking him round this evening. AVS approving, we went to Matins at St Michael's and walked on to No. 67 Hornsey Lane, where we enquired for Mr Sangar.

That gentleman, hearing my voice, came out, and looked pleased to see us. He came for a stroll in Waterlow Park; we talked about the strike and what job Rex could do: "Shovel coal or something". We dropped Helen at the Grove and continued our stroll down Fitzroy Park.

In spite of sunshine and gay people, it was not a cheerful walk; we were both depressed. However, Rex said again that he would come down to Stogumber, and we *tried* to be cheerful.

On our way to the Rossettis AVS and I enquired for the latest news at a paper shop. The very nice man said that nothing was known for certain yet, but he would strongly advise us to travel as he felt sure there would be a strike. So we posted various cards about our return, and took a 'bus to Regents Park.

It *was* nice to see Miss Rossetti again at No. 3 St Edmunds Terrace. She has been in Rome for two years, but there she was, lying in her chair in the dining room, with the Rossetti and Madox Brown pictures looking down from the walls, as if the two years had never been.

89

One remembers her smile and serenity so much more clearly than her affliction that it is a shock to see again how contorted and crippled she is. Rheumatoid Arthritis attacked her suddenly when she was an athletic young girl, and now she can't leave her chair without help, and once put on her poor deformed feet, can only just shuffle along. AVS, who went to look after her in Rome years ago, always holds her up as the greatest possible example of courage.

Although her father Mr William Michael is dead – it must be quite seven years ago – I still expect him to come in from his library for tea, with his piercing black eyes, white beard, and velvet skull cap. He always greeted me with a grave courtesy that impressed me greatly as a little girl: "Ah, Robert Garnett's daughter! It is always a pleasure, more, a privilege" (here he used to bow over my hand) "to welcome a member of that illustrious family – in the very house in which your distinguished grandfather resided for many years."*

Imogen,† Miss Rossetti's niece, is still in Rome, but her friend Molly Tapper was there, as plump and cheerful as ever. She and I descended to the basement and got the tea. We stayed till about 6.15 and Molly kindly sent off a wire to Stogumber to say we were arriving tomorrow.

As we were talking to Father in the study on our return to West Hill, the door opened and a voice said "Oh, there is someone home after all". There stood Narney, slim and pink and white and very pretty under a large blue hat. But very cross too: "What fools you are to let the fire out" was her next remark.

I hastily lit it, while she told us that, hearing we were in town, she had availed herself of a day-off to see us. When we explained that we were leaving tomorrow she was *not* pleased.

While the floodgates of her wrath were opening I fled downstairs to get supper. A delicious one had been left ready in the larder by Miss Love. And the study fire burnt up; also, to further appease Narney, AVS said we would catch a later train.

So when Rex came he and I were sent to the Highgate Road to countermand our taxi and order a later one. This meant another evening walk, a warm sunset paling behind the dusky Parliament Fields.

We found Dicky and Norman Dimmock eating their supper on our return, ravenously hungry after a day's motoring. Rex joined them, and afterwards we all helped clear away, and sat round the table –

* William Michael Rossetti, brother of the Pre-Raphaelite poet and painter Dante Gabriel Rossetti, took over No. 3 St Edmund's Terrace from Richard Garnett and his family on their removal to live at the British Musuem.

† A life-long friend of Anne's, she married Geoffrey Dennis, the novelist.

Dicky, Norman, AVS, Narney, and Rex and I, telling funny stories. These soon changed to horrors, of which Narney had a good store, operations that went wrong, etc., at the Radcliffe. Thrills were chiefly related by Norman, who experienced plenty in the RAF.

About 10 o'clock he and Dicky left; the rest of us sat round the gas fire eating cherries and oranges. So passed my last night at West Hill.

CHAPTER VIII

May 3rd – May 27th, 1926

❧❧❀ ❀❧❀

*M*AY 3rd. The taxi came about 11.0, and Narney accompanied us to Paddington. There had been a mistake about our train; there was none till 1.30. Narney had to have some lunch, so she and I found an ABC, where I nursed a little black kitten, and had an ice myself.

It was well that we were early, for Paddington was crammed, everyone like ourselves rushing out of London while they could. Our train was in and we settled ourselves, and saw Narney to the last as she awaited her train across the line; we could lean out of the window and talk to her.

About a quarter of an hour before the start, three ladies bundled into our carriage, with a hundred-and-one wraps, packages, rugs, and fur coats. The eldest, a determined old girl with black eyes and white hair, said, or rather shouted: "Is this train right for Crowcombe? Can anyone tell me?" and issued commands as to her bundles, with a stream of comments on the strike, the absence of newspapers, and the state of the nation. I thought she must be the Hon. Mrs Trollope of Crowcombe Court at least.

When we returned from our lunch she was spiritedly guarding our seats against an invading mob; so we thanked her, and fell into conversation.

She was a Mrs Headlam, and lives on Crowcombe Heathfield with her niece. A great horsewoman in her time, and they both paint. So we soon became bosom friends and talked the whole way. Mrs Headlam lamented the good old days when 'the gentry' could afford to keep hunters and hosts of servants, and the main roads were fit for horses.

The name seemed familiar and at last I remembered Ned talking of two ladies on the Heathfield who spent all their time sketching and were on that account suspected of being German spies.

We arrived at Stogumber in brilliant sunshine, and there was Sully to meet us. The meadows were vividly green and sheeted with buttercups, the hedges full of tall cow-parsley, bluebells in the copses and birds singing everywhere.

At Manor Farm Mrs Redd, a stout, rosy, motherly woman, came out to meet us. She had tea ready, of clotted cream, strawberry jam, and home-made butter. Manor Farm is a typical farmhouse with a delicious farmy, country smell; it has large rooms with low ceilings and uneven floors. Our sitting-room opens through french windows to a daised lawn with a weeping ash and a monkey-puzzle tree.

Dear old Miss Hall came in and sat talking to us while we unpacked. I think we shall like being in the village again.

May 4th.   I had a warm welcome at Bicknoller, where I hurried as fast as I could after breakfast. It is not such a pretty walk as from Brewers Water. Filbert was already saddled ready for me and Mr Frost rode with me up Weacombe. He was very jovial and teased me unmercifully about "Someone I was keen on." And this though I have never said there was anyone special!

After walking home to change, he came to drive me to Polo. I squashed into the car with his mother. She was very affable, and apparently delighted to have me back in Somerset.

I had noticed AVS rather on a high-horse one day after having had tea with her; apparently the lady had remarked "What a nice little pair Anne and dear Duddles make, riding together". I hope AVS was not too glarey.

Duddles was playing very well on his mare Jane, and the Captain on Marco, in a practice game for green ponies. Suddenly Mrs Frost cried: "Oh heavens! Dudley's hurt!" and we saw him sitting on the ground with Winter pouring water over his knee. I was sent to find out what had happened, and if it was his bad leg. "It was nothing – got a ball just below the knee". He went back to play, but soon dismounted and changed places with the Captain, who was by then umpiring. But at the end of the chukka he came in. His mother again sent me to tell him to take his boot off, adding "Don't let him think I'm fussing."

He came limping over and reclined in the front seat while Winter pulled off his boot, and confided to me that he felt so sick while playing that he feared he'd fall off in a dead faint, adding to Mrs Frost "For God's sake don't fuss!" The poor little woman had not said much, but was fidgety. No wonder, she has had enough trouble with his legs; he broke an ankle at Harrow, and there was a bad accident in the Argentine when a pony rolled on him, breaking a leg in six places.

He drove us home using only one foot, wincing at every move. Dr Ollerhead, who had sent the offending ball, came and examined him

93

before we left and said he thought no bone was broken.

Very unwillingly, he sat in the car at the stables and let me do the watering and see to the ponies. Then the Captain drove him home.

May 6th. There are no trains as yet, though we hear that there may be two tomorrow. But they will be of no use for school, so I shall have to board there till the strike is over – What a beastly nuisance – no riding! Mr Frost is to go into Minehead Cottage Hospital tomorrow, to be X-rayed, and will probably be kept there a few days.

May 7th. AVS has been urging me to ride to see Mrs Headlam, but I have not been able to do so till today. I took Milly, through heavy storms, along the wooded lanes. The trees are all in leaf, with bluebells and primroses below. Torrents of rain fell at intervals but they made the sunshine between even brighter as it flashed on the wet leaves. And there was a delicious smell of wet leaf-mould.

Two amiable carters issued directions as to the whereabouts of Mrs Headlam: "You must go on up thicky road along ways; t'won't take vive minutes, vor certain, if 'ee trots on fast, then ee'll zee a little green lane on the right, but don't take no notice of 'ee. Bear left, and then you'll zee a gurt covert, and the house be on the corner of 'ee."

Duly taking no notice of the little green lane, I arrived at the great covert, though in fact the whole way was wooded. A red roof showed between the trees, and I led Mildmay into a very pretty garden.

I was welcomed by the niece, who knew all about me, and helped me tie Milly to a post. The cottage was so nice inside – books and papers everywhere and good pictures. Mrs Headlam came downstairs and greeted me warmly; they pressed me to stay for lunch, and came out to see me off, promising to visit us soon.

May 8th. I took a lift with the Evans Smiths, going to Polo, and walked on to Minehead to visit Duddles. He appeared very bored, in a small attic at the top of the hospital. His mother was with him and begged me to come again; I said I would be able to while boarding at school, and returned to Dunster in time to watch the last chukkas.

AVS and I spent the evening in copying out wireless reports that AVS had listened to on the Sully's wireless, and took them to the Post Office where they were displayed in the window. My idea, as it is being done at Bicknoller.

People warmly approved and gathered to read them. There are very few newspapers now and even those have only one sheet.

May 10th. There were two trains today and I went to school on the first. Everything seemed as usual apart from a policeman at each

94

People gathered to read them

station, strangers as driver and stoker, and a fat old gentleman in civilian clothes as guard. The train was only a quarter of an hour late which everyone thought surprisingly good, and better than during the last coal-strike when the trains could only crawl, owing to foreign coal.

To my disgust there were only three girls at school. But perhaps I shall be able to do some hard work in such peace.

May 14th.   Home again; how thankful I am to leave school. It was really dull boarding there, as so few girls could get back, and no Miss Webster. My forms for the School Certificate exam. had been delayed too, by the strike, and poor Miss Benison [one of the mistresses] had to go to Taunton for them.

I spent this first day of liberty at Elworthy, and stayed to milk Brindle, getting her quite dry which made me proud, as I have not milked for a long time. I like milking, pressing my head against the soft, sweet-smelling flank, warm teats in my hands, and the jets spurting into the shining pail where a creamy froth rises.

Mrs Hayes solemnly produced a bottle of ginger wine and three glasses and we drank each other's health before I left. Somehow I reached Stogumber in fifteen minutes. I ran most of the way up Mondsborough, and then it is all downhill. We went to the Sully's to listen to the wireless. They have a loud-speaker and we heard Thomas' speech, which I thought a trifle too saintly, and then to the terms on which the Railway Companies agree to take back the men. Then the Union's statement, which was largely Humble Pie.

May 17th.   Trains are still uncertain, but the 8.45 ran this morning; it was a glorious day too, fresh and cool, the dew lying on the long lush grass and buttercups. I felt it a great waste to be going to school.

At Williton Chris, the stationmaster's son got in; he thought the strike "the blooming limit, I've cycled a good 250 miles and am fed

95

up." At any rate, I am not to board at school again; AVS thinks I look pale for lack of fresh air.

May 22nd. A very hot day. The Evans Smiths were at a belated breakfast when I arrived. Things are hectic at the stable as Mr Frost is still disabled and Paul's successor has been taken suddenly ill with a strained heart and has had to go home. So the Captain and Winter have to deal with eleven ponies. A friend of theirs, Miss Lee Michell, is coming to help in a few days.*

I did some grooming, a mighty job as the ponies played yesterday and the sweat had dried on them. By the time I had finished I was in a lather myself and the colour of a beetroot. Mr Frost, cleaning tack in the harness room, looked as cool as his name. We had a violent squabble because I took a pair of leathers that he wanted to clean; to appease him I promised to clean them myself. To make amends, when I returned from riding he said he would drive me home. It was so hot that I was most grateful – but when we got to his car a tyre was flat, so I lunched with him and his mother. She was most kind, taking me upstairs to a cool, airy bedroom and putting clean towels and powder at my disposal.

May 24th. I found Miss Lee Michell at the stables and took my orders from her. She is a pretty girl with skin tanned golden-brown. She has very blue eyes and bobbed curly golden-brown hair. We grew very hot grooming and saddling up; to cool down I rode without coat or hat like Miss Michell; she says she never wears a hat in the country. The Captain, who rode Marco out with us, was much amused and called us his beauty-chorus.

Mr Frost was hobbling about the yard doing odd jobs on our return, and invited me to change at his lodgings, as they were taking me to Polo, not at Dunster, but at the Taunton Vale Club.

We packed ourselves into the car; there was an argument because Duddles refused to wear his new hat. His mother is always 'at him' about his clothes and expressed the fear that he is growing slovenly here. To this her son replied that he is *working* here, and in any case, if people only cared for his clothes and not for him, he is damned if he'll ever go to a damned tea-fight or a damned dance again, etc. This effectually silenced poor Mrs Frost.

We stopped in Taunton to enquire the way from a small urchin, who said he was going to Orchard Portman himself. "Jump up then, we'll take you". A broad grin appeared and then faded.

"But me brother's coming too", said the urchin – crestfallen. "All right, I'll take your brother too", said Duddles cheerfully. Another

* Anne's acquaintance with Constance Lee Michell was to prove fateful.

96

urchin appeared and climbed into the dicky, identical with the first but one size smaller. We had not gone far when a sad little voice was heard: "You see, Sir, I've another brother, and we were going to pick him up on the way". Mr Frost, who has unlimited confidence in the capacity of his dicky, replied that that was all right, and we stopped at a cottage for another smaller-sized urchin. "How many more brothers have you?" "That's the lot, sir" was the reply, and we lost no more time in getting to the ground.

A very good game was enlivened by Major Campbell tearing after a ball he had shot to the wrong goal. There was a mighty shout of "Wrong Way! Wrong Way!" but he paid no heed till he had nearly reached the goal. He then reined up, looking rather sheepish, and there was a roar of laughter.

May 27th. In the train today was an earnest young man with all the statistics of the coal strike at his finger-ends. Miss Ford's friend the Railway Inspector, who is a Conservative, was in the carriage and had a great time arguing with this youth, a Labour supporter. Much time and trouble was spent by him in quoting facts and figures to prove that the miners are hardly done by – which none of us doubt for a moment. Where we differed was his belief that the Tories wish to trample the poor in the dust and keep the working-classes down, meanwhile pouring gold into the pockets of dukes and earls.

We often play Bridge in the train now, Chris, Miss Smith, Miss Ford and I making the four. Yesterday as Chris was absent, a railway-ganger kindly took his place; I made Grand Slam in No trumps.

AVS and I both had letters today; mine from Father, hers from Mother. I skimmed through mine; it said that he wants me to live at West Hill when I leave school. The significance of this did not dawn on me till I read 'After Christmas you will return to Highgate and learn drawing. No doubt you will miss your riding, but there are compensations in town life.'

I do not want to live at home one bit! But it is evident that Father's mind is made up. In her letter Mother says she has done her best to dissuade him but it is hopeless. Ugh! I wish I had known this before I had dreamt the lovely dream of living with AVS in a cottage here. . .

EPILOGUE

*T*HE 'lovely dream' came true in part, for AVS got her cottage. In order to start an art school training Anne returned to live in London in December 1926, when she ended her diary. She described her last months in the Quantock country as vividly as the period covered by *Caught From Time*, for she savoured each precious moment before her time ran out. After it had done so, she came back to AVS for holidays, which it transpired were only the prelude to the rest of her life in West Somerset.

Richard Garnett, his Children and Grandchildren

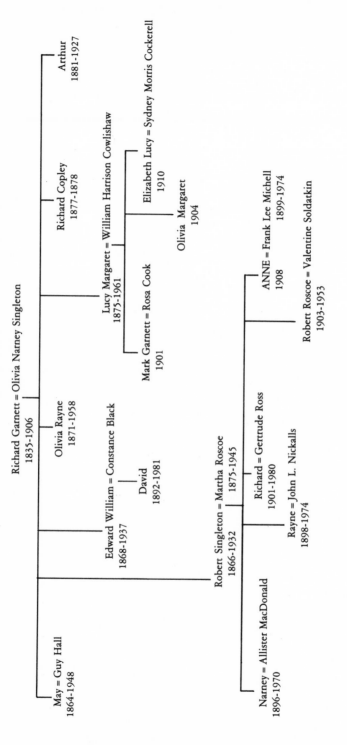